Calling All Cats!

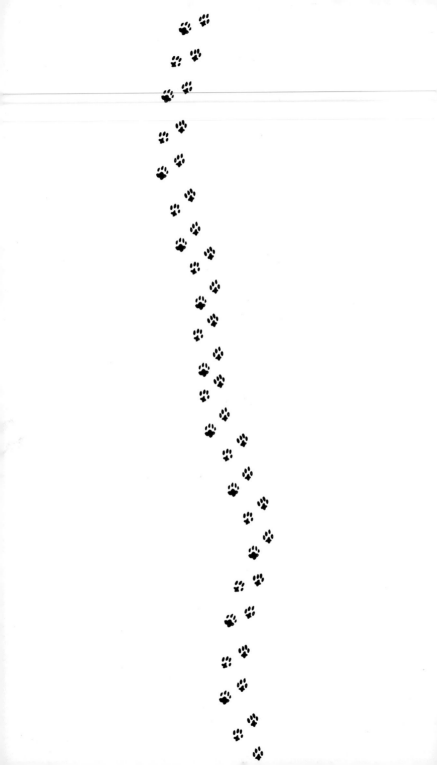

Calling All Cats!

PURRRFECT NAMES
for Your
FABULOUS FELINE

Joanne O'Sullivan

LARK BOOKS

A Division of Sterling Publishing Co., Inc.
New York / London

Library of Congress Cataloging-in-Publication Data

O'Sullivan, Joanne.
  Calling all cats! : purrrfect names for your fabulous feline / Joanne
O'Sullivan. -- 1st ed.
     p. cm.
  Includes index.
  ISBN-13: 978-1-60059-265-2 (pb-trade pbk. : alk. paper)
  ISBN-10: 1-60059-265-1 (pb-trade pbk. : alk. paper)
  1. Cats--Names. I. Title.
  SF442.4.O88 2008
  636.8--dc22

                                        2007042181

10 9 8 7 6 5 4 3 2 1

First Edition

Published by Lark Books, A Division of
Sterling Publishing Co., Inc.
387 Park Avenue South, New York, N.Y. 10016

Text © 2008, Lark Books
Illustrations © 2007, Susan McBride

Distributed in Canada by Sterling Publishing,
c/o Canadian Manda Group, 165 Dufferin Street
Toronto, Ontario, Canada M6K 3H6

Distributed in the United Kingdom by GMC Distribution Services,
Castle Place, 166 High Street, Lewes, East Sussex, England BN7 1XU

Distributed in Australia by Capricorn Link (Australia) Pty Ltd.,
P.O. Box 704, Windsor, NSW 2756 Australia

If you have questions or comments about this book, please contact:
Lark Books
67 Broadway
Asheville, NC 28801
(828) 253-0467

Manufactured in China

ISBN-13: 978-1-60059-265-2
ISBN-10: 1-60059-265-1

For information about custom editions, special sales, premium and
corporate purchases, please contact Sterling Special Sales Department at
800-805-5489 or specialsales@sterlingpub.com.

DEVELOPMENT EDITOR:
Deborah Morgenthal

ART DIRECTOR
AND ILLUSTRATOR:
Susan McBride

COVER DESIGNER:
Cindy LaBreacht

EDITORIAL ASSISTANCE:
Kathleen McCafferty

Calling All Cats!

CONTENTS

Introduction

There's a new presence in your house: a fascinating and mysterious member of the family. Whether she's purring in your lap or chasing a shadow on the wall, this independent-minded creature adds a special dimension to your life. But what exactly is your cat's name?

Cats are so expressive, and some say so complex. They're at once domesticated and a little bit wild, affectionate and, a minute later, aloof. And kittens! Well, you could spend hours entertained by the antics of those darling creatures.

Choosing a name that captures the elusive essence of your cat or kitten might seem daunting...and perhaps a bit pointless: do cats really come when you call them? They're so different from dogs (in so many ways!), who eagerly await the sound of a human calling their name. But, regardless of how consistently your cat comes to you when called, naming your cat well symbolizes the bond between you two; it's a clear signal that you belong to her, and—although not all cats will admit this publicly—that she belongs to you!

- ❏ Attila
- ❏ Bill the Cat
- ✔ Bella
- ❏ Bête Noir
- ❏ Bucky Katt
- ❏ Boom Boom Pussini
- ❏ Captain Amerikat
- ❏ Catbert

- ✔ Nero
- ❏ Neville
- ❏ Prince
- ❏ Paganini
- ❏ Puccini
- ❏ Rachmaninoff
- ❏ Rossini

- ❏ Puma
- ✔ Pyewacket
- ❏ Rufus
- ❏ Sassie

Adding to the challenge is the endless number of names to choose from: she soft, she's fluffy—but does that mean her name should be Fluffy? He's playful—are you looking at a Frisky? He leaves artistic paw print patterns on your carpet—is he a Pollock? That's why this book is so handy. It will help you explore your options, organize your thinking, and help you choose one name that strikes the right note, paints the perfect picture, and sums up that certain something that makes your cat the utterly unique creature he is.

HOW TO USE THIS BOOK

f you're lucky, you'll be living with your cat for up to 15 years. It's worth your effort to approach the naming process thoughtfully. Spend time getting to know your cat before choosing a name. Observe her personality, her energy, her style, and physical characteristics. But don't spend too much time. Many a cat owner, lost in contemplation and rumination, has ended up with a cat permanently called Cat or Kitty.

Chances are that if you're reading this book, you're also looking for a name with some meaning, some flair, something that reflects your interests or your worldview. What defines *you*? Your love of music, art, or history? Your wine connoisseurship? Your sense of humor? Your profession? Do you like the drama of a unique, attention-grabbing name, or do you prefer something subtle and classic?

Look through the book. Some people are skimmers and scanners who flip through and find a name that just *feels* right. Others will methodically read every name, make lists and charts, and conduct informal polls of friends and relations to find the perfect match. Still others fall somewhere in between. Use the boxes next to each name to check the ones you're interested in or to create a list if you're that type, or just say the names out loud.

Now you've got all the information you need to start matching a name to your pet. You might have decided that you'll definitely name your cat after an artist. That's a good start, but is your cat a Basquiat or a Botticelli? That's where the chemistry of a good name kicks in: assessing your cat's looks and personality will help you get the right fit. If, like many cat lovers, you find yourself with several cats to name at once, consider pairs or trios of names that relate: Apples and Oranges. Bright Eyes and Bushy Tail. Wynken, Blynken, and Nod.

Lean toward names with a more lasting quality. While choosing a trendy name may give you instant cache, you may end up regretting it years down the road when your cat is still going strong, but her name seems stale and dated.

Try saying the name out loud repeatedly. Say it in different volumes and with different speeds. Does the name trip from the tongue or trip you up? This "test drive" can help you narrow your options. While you may select something fancy like Princess Fifi de la Bourgogne de Borghese, you will, for your own sake and your cat's, inevitably end up shortening it for daily use. Names with two or three syllables are easier for you to say and for your cat to recognize. It's OK if you end up calling your princess Fifi. You and she both know about her title—that's what really counts.

It might sound a little kooky, but ask your cat what she thinks. Test the name with her and observe how she responds. If she doesn't react or looks away, you may have to try again. If she approaches you, or her body language shows she's pleased, you may have a winner.

Registering A Cat Name

If you purchase a pedigreed cat from a cattery, your pet may already have a 'cattery name'. That is the name that the breeder chose and registered with the Cat Fancier's Association. Cattery names must be unique—in other words, there must be no other cat registered with the same name. There are very specific rules about naming. Given names, such as Ann or Maria, can't be used, nor can titles such as Princess or Monsieur. Names must be at least two letters and must be truly distinctive from other cat names. In other words, Tom or Ginger isn't going to cut it. And changing the spelling of a name or adding an 's' to make it *appear* different doesn't count. If you want to find out more about cattery names and see a list of registered names, consult the Cat Fancier's Association web site at: http://www.cfa.org/org/registration.html#rules.

CAT CALLS

"Why even bother to call a cat?" some skeptics ask. "He won't come—unless he was already planning to anyway."

Au contraire. Different cats respond to being called in different ways. Some cats instinctively come running when you call. Others seem disinterested in whatever it is that you're yammering on about. If your cat falls into this camp, don't fret. Cats can be trained to respond to your calls. But being the analytical creatures that they are, they need to know "What's my motivation?" Your job is to supply them with one: invariably it will be food or a favored toy.

It's best to start your cat-calling training when your cat is young. Pick times when he's is in a good mood and will be most responsive to your attempts to modify him. Older cats can be trained in this way, too (just don't let on that you're "training" them!). The key is positive reinforcement: reward your cat when she does something you want her to do, in this case, coming when you call her name.

To build a foundation for training, you'll need to talk to your cat or kitten as often as you can to get her used to the sound of your voice and the idea that talking is the way you communicate. Your cat should start to associate the sound of your voice with pleasant things, such as being rubbed or getting a treat. This can seem tricky, especially when you may be at the same time trying to train her to stay off the couch. One way you can avoid confusing your cat is to not use her name when you're trying to train her *not* to do things. For example, say, "Off the couch!" and move her, rather than yell, "Off the couch, Isis!"

Choose a special treat that will only be given to her when she comes when called. Give this tidbit a special name; then, when she hears "nibbles," for example, she'll know that something good is about to happen.

Now you're ready to start practicing. Take the treat in your hand, or put it in your cat's bowl. Say the name of the treat. Your cat will approach you and take the treat. Say the word again after she's eaten the treat. Pet her and give her lots of affection.

Continue this training at least once a day for about five days to a week. If you're consistent, your cat will really start to get the picture.
Repeat the process using a second treat. Don't forget the petting. Then walk away. More than likely your cat will follow you. When she does, say the special treat name and her name before giving her another treat. She will start to associate the two words with happy events.

Once your cat is consistently responding to the words, it's time to start withdrawing the treats. You'll find that your cat will not stop coming because the treats have disappeared—she'll still associate the words with positive experiences. And just because you stop giving treats doesn't mean you should stop the petting and affection. That will come to be your cat's reward for responding to your calls. The next step is to gradually withdraw using the treat name and use only the cat's name. And there you have it—your cat is coming when called.

Will this work for all cats? It should, if you're consistent. Give it a try, and see if it works for you. If it doesn't, see Here Kitty, Kitty on page 14 for alternative methods that people swear brings a cat running to them every time.

Here, Kitty, Kitty

If "Here, Sweet Pea, come to Mama" isn't working, try one or more of the following approaches.

The first is the tried-and-true cat call that's been used for generations: "*Here, kitty, kitty*" or "Here, kitty, kitty, kitty, kitty." Many people find themselves calling their cats in this way without consciously knowing why.

There may be something to the here-kitty-kitty pattern. Some studies show that when cats hear a "t" and "k" sound, their animal nature kicks in. The t-k combination reminds them of the chirp of a bird, it's said, and hearing it brings out the predator in them and brings them running. Some people even skip the words and simply repeat a "tchk tchk tchk," finding that it brings results. In countries around the world, regardless of the language spoken, cats seem to respond consistently to these sounds. Repetition, it would seem, is important, though. Most bird songs consist of sounds in sequences, often of three or five sounds grouped together. That could be why 'Here kitty, kitty" or "Here kitty, kitty, kitty, kitty" have evolved as the most universal cat-calling patterns.

Studies also show that feline hearing is attuned to much higher sound frequencies than human hearing. While the squeak of a mouse is often inaudible to us, cats can hear it loud and clear. This special attribute may help your cat catch prey, but can it help you when you're trying to get your cat to come? Some cats respond to their names only when the pitch of the voice is modulated toward the higher end of the spectrum. Many cats also answer to a repeated whistle for the same reason. Others come running when a repeated "kissing" sound is made.

If none of these methods works for you, there's still a fail-safe: Nary a cat in the world won't magically appear when summoned by the sound of his dry food shaking in its box or the siren call of a can opener slicing into that tin container of delectable minced tuna.

Glamour Pusses

Sleek, confident, effortlessly elegant— is there any creature quite as glamorous as a cat? Choose a name to capture the certain JE NE SAIS QUOI that makes your kitty the fascinating feline he or she is, that certain 1940s film star flair. These are the CRÈME DE LA CRÈME of cat names. Doesn't your pet deserve the very best?

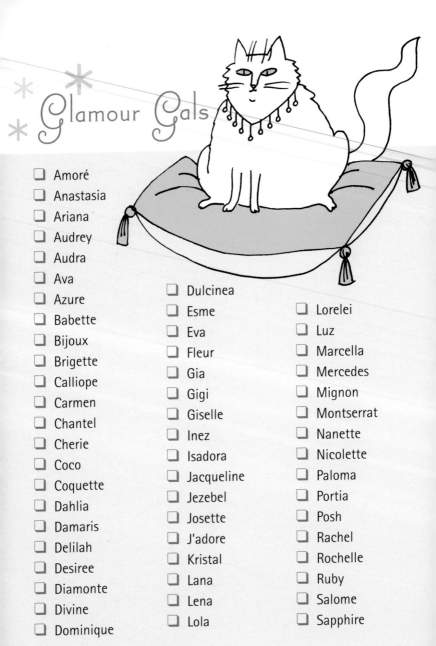

Glamour Gals

- ❏ Amoré
- ❏ Anastasia
- ❏ Ariana
- ❏ Audrey
- ❏ Audra
- ❏ Ava
- ❏ Azure
- ❏ Babette
- ❏ Bijoux
- ❏ Brigette
- ❏ Calliope
- ❏ Carmen
- ❏ Chantel
- ❏ Cherie
- ❏ Coco
- ❏ Coquette
- ❏ Dahlia
- ❏ Damaris
- ❏ Delilah
- ❏ Desiree
- ❏ Diamonte
- ❏ Divine
- ❏ Dominique

- ❏ Dulcinea
- ❏ Esme
- ❏ Eva
- ❏ Fleur
- ❏ Gia
- ❏ Gigi
- ❏ Giselle
- ❏ Inez
- ❏ Isadora
- ❏ Jacqueline
- ❏ Jezebel
- ❏ Josette
- ❏ J'adore
- ❏ Kristal
- ❏ Lana
- ❏ Lena
- ❏ Lola

- ❏ Lorelei
- ❏ Luz
- ❏ Marcella
- ❏ Mercedes
- ❏ Mignon
- ❏ Montserrat
- ❏ Nanette
- ❏ Nicolette
- ❏ Paloma
- ❏ Portia
- ❏ Posh
- ❏ Rachel
- ❏ Rochelle
- ❏ Ruby
- ❏ Salome
- ❏ Sapphire

Glamour Guys

- Satine
- Scarlett
- Sheba
- Silvie
- Solange
- Sonya
- Stella
- Tatiana
- Titiana
- Topaz
- Velvet
- Venus
- Violetta
- Vivian
- Zsa Zsa

- Alistair
- Adrian
- Amedeo
- Amadeus
- Andre
- Aramis
- Archer
- Armand
- Ascot
- Balthazar
- Blaise
- Cary
- Castle
- Charlton
- Christo
- Christophe
- Conrad
- Cordovan
- Dante
- Didi
- Dougray
- Emile
- Fabio
- Falcon

- Florian
- Francois
- Giorgio
- Guillaume
- Heath
- Henri
- Jean-Paul
- Lazar
- Lazlo
- Leland
- Marcel
- Maximillian
- Montgomery
- Nico
- Olivier
- Omar
- Ranier
- Randolph
- René
- Roman
- Romeo
- Placido
- Prospero
- Xavier

Great Purrformances

The camera loves a cat—those gorgeous eyes, that luxurious fur. It's no wonder cats are often seen on the screen, in movies and on television. Who can forget Mr. Bigglesworth, the sly lap cat of the AUSTIN POWERS' Dr. Evil? Or Pyewacket, the familiar who helped enchant Jimmy Stewart in BELL, BOOK, AND CANDLE? Maybe one of these names will capture your cat's star quality.

The Big Screen

NAME	FILM
❑ 17	*Dr. Shrinker*
❑ Alpha	*Cat Women of the Moon*
❑ Angus	*Jinxed!*
❑ Annoying Customer	*Clerks*
❑ Ayatollah	*Diva*
❑ Babe	*Enemy of the State*
❑ Bad Luck	*They Were Expendable*
❑ Beeswax	*Her Alibi*
❑ Binks	*Hocus Pocus*
❑ Bob	*One Fine Day*
❑ Burbank	*Lethal Weapon*
❑ Cat	*Breakfast at Tiffany's*
❑ Catzilla	*Mouse Hunt*
❑ Church	*Pet Sematary*
❑ Cleavis	*Sleepwalkers*
❑ Clovis	*Sleepwalkers*
❑ Coco	*Jungle 2 Jungle*
❑ Cosmic Creepers	*Bedknobs and Broomsticks*
❑ D.C.	*That Darn Cat*
❑ Dandilo	*The Fly*
❑ Elmyra	*Children of the Corn II: The Final Sacrifice*
❑ Fellini	*Breaking Away*
❑ General	*Cat's Eye*
❑ General Sterling Price	*True Grit*
❑ Gris-Gris	*When The Cat's Away*
❑ Heathcliff	*Touch and Go*
❑ Hobby	*Birdy*

NAME	FILM
❏ Jackson	*The Crawling Hand*
❏ Jake	*The Cat From Outer Space*
❏ Jarvis	*The Man With Two Brains*
❏ Jones	*Alien*
❏ Lambda	*Cat Women of the Moon*
❏ Lucy-Belle	*The Cat From Outer Space*
❏ Madcat	*Inspector Gadget*
❏ Matilda	*The Stars Fell on Henrietta*
❏ Midnight	*Catwoman*
❏ Milo	*The Adventures of Milo and Otis*
❏ Miss Kitty	*Batman Returns*
❏ Mr. Bigglesworth	The *Austin Powers* movies
❏ Mr. Jinx	*Meet the Fockers*
❏ Mr. Tinkles	*Cats and Dogs*
❏ Muffy	*Mars Attacks!*
❏ Gatto Nero	*The Black Cat*
❏ Neutron	*This Island Earth*
❏ Orion	*Men in Black*
❏ Pearl	*Assassins*
❏ P.J.	*Pajama Game*
❏ Princess Leah Lucky Buttons	*Go*
❏ Puma	*Ring of Terror*
❏ Pyewacket	*Bell, Book, and Candle*
❏ Rufus	*The Re-Animator*
❏ Sassie	*Homeward Bound: The Incredible Journey*

NAME	FILM
☐ Snowbell	*Stuart Little*
☐ Solomon	*You Only Live Twice*
☐ Sweetie	*The Fifth Element*
☐ Tao	*The Incredible Journey*
☐ Thomasina	*The Three Lives of Thomasina*
☐ Tiny	*Unlawful Entry*
☐ Tonto	*Harry and Tonto*
☐ Tullia	*The Eye of the Cat*
☐ Whitey	*Stage Door*
☐ Winky	*Escape to Witch Mountain*
☐ Zeta	*Cat Women of the Moon*

Movie Characters That Aren't Cats

NAME	MOVIE
☆ Annie Hall	*Annie Hall*
☆ Baby Jane	*Whatever Happened to Baby Jane?*
☆ Big Lebowski	*The Big Lebowski*
☆ Bond	The *James Bond* movies
☆ Cabiria	*Nights of Cabiria*
☆ Catwoman	Batman Returns
☆ Cypher	*The Matrix*
☆ E.T.	*E.T.*
☆ Fanny Brice	*Funny Girl*
☆ Frenchie	*Destry Rides Again*
☆ Gidget	The *Gidget* movies
☆ Holly Golightly	*Breakfast at Tiffany's*
☆ Foxy Brown	*Foxy Brown*
☆ Louise	*Thelma and Louise*
☆ M	The *James Bond* movies
☆ Maude	*Harold and Maude*
☆ Mifune	*The Matrix*
☆ Mad Max	*Mad Max*
☆ Miss Moneypenny	The *James Bond* movies
☆ Morpheus	*The Matrix*
☆ Mrs. Incredible	*The Incredibles*
☆ Mr. Moto	*Mr. Moto*
☆ Mr. Tibbs	*In The Heat of The Night*
☆ Neo	*The Matrix*
☆ Octopussy	*Octopussy*
☆ Ninotchka	*Ninotchka*
☆ Princess Leia	The *Star Wars* Movies
☆ Pussy Galore	*Goldfinger*
☆ Ripley	*Alien*
☆ Q	The *James Bond* movies
☆ Scarlett	*Gone with the Wind*
☆ Sparky Pilastry	*Bring It On*
☆ Thelma	*Thelma and Louise*
☆ Trinity	*The Matrix*
☆ Wonka	*Willy Wonka and the Chocolate Factory*
☆ Yoda	The *Star Wars* Movies

The Little Screen

NAME	SHOW
☐ Bonkers	*All My Children*
☐ Cool Cat	*Pee Wee's Playhouse*
☐ Boo-Boo Kitty	*Laverne and Shirley*
☐ Clinker	*Perry Mason*
☐ Cyclops	*Cold Case*
☐ Dalton The Wonder Cat	*My Litter Box Was Dirty*
☐ Fluffy	*The Brady Bunch*
☐ Fondue	*Kablam! Sniz and Fondie*
☐ Frankenstein	*Red Dwarf*
☐ Grandpere	*Mr. Rogers' Neighborhood*
☐ Eric the Cat	*Monty Python's Flying Circus*
☐ Henrietta Pussycat	*Mr. Rogers' Neighborhood*
☐ Isis	*Star Trek*
☐ Jack	*Blue Peter*
☐ Jason	*Blue Peter*
☐ Jill	*Blue Peter*
☐ Kit	*Charmed*
☐ Kari	*Blue Peter*
☐ Koolio	*Friends*
☐ Lucky	*Alf*
☐ Marmalade	*The Beverly Hillbillies*
☐ Midnight	*Mannix, Barnaby Jones*

NAME	SHOW
❏ Minerva	*Our Miss Brooks*
❏ Miss Kitty Fantastico	*Buffy the Vampire Slayer*
❏ Nelix	*Star Trek: Voyager*
❏ Mr. Piddles	*The L Word*
❏ Myrtle	*The X Files*
❏ Oke	*Blue Peter*
❏ Olivia	*Cold Case*
❏ Panther	*Early Edition*
❏ Pequita	*Seinfeld*
❏ Rusty	*The Beverly Hillbillies*
❏ Salem Saberhagen	*Sabrina the Teen Witch*
❏ Sam	*Bonanza*
❏ Salty	*Caroline in the City*
❏ Sizzle	*The Puzzle Place*
❏ Smelly Cat	*Friends*
❏ Snicklefritz	*The Big Comfy Couch*
❏ Sniz	*Kablam!/Sniz and Fondie*
❏ Snow's Cat	*Early Edition*
❏ Spot	*Star Trek: Generations*
❏ Tiddles	*Are You Being Served?*
❏ Toonces	*Saturday Night Live*
❏ Tripod	*Cold Case*

TV Characters That Aren't Cats

NAME	SHOW
☆ Alfalfa	*Our Gang*
☆ Beeker	*The Muppet Show*
☆ Buffy	*Buffy the Vampire Slayer*
☆ Carmela	*The Sopranos*
☆ Costanza	*Seinfeld*
☆ Elmo	*Sesame Street*
☆ Frasier	*Frasier*
☆ Gilligan	*Gilligan's Island*
☆ Gomer	*Gomer Pyle*
☆ Gomez	*The Addams Family*
☆ Kermit	*The Muppet Show*
☆ Lurch	*The Addams Family*
☆ Monk	*Monk*
☆ Morticia	*The Addams Family*
☆ Mulder	*The X Files*
☆ Opie	*The Andy Griffith Show*
☆ Sabrina	*Sabrina the Teen Witch*
☆ Scully	*The X-Files*
☆ Spock	*Star Trek*
☆ Tonto	*The Lone Ranger*
☆ Xena	*Xena: Warrior Princess*

Lions and Panthers and Leopards, Oh My!

Fabulous felines, larger than life (and larger than the average house cat), these celebrity big cats had big roles to play on TV and in the movies.

NAME	MEDIA
☆ Charlemagne	Lion puppet on *The Morning Show*
☆ Chauncey	Cougar who appeared in TV commercials
☆ Clarence	Lion from *Daktari/Clarence The Cross-Eyed Lion*
☆ Daniel Tiger	*Mister Rogers' Neighborhood*
☆ Dreyfus	Lion from TV commercials
☆ Drooper	*The Banana Splits*
☆ Frasier	Lion from *Frasier the Sensuous Lion*
☆ Freddie	Played Clarence in *Datktari/ Clarence The Cross-Eyed Lion*
☆ Heller	Cougar from TV commercials and *Shazam!*
☆ Jackie	One of the MGM movie studio mascot lions
☆ Leonora	Girl who turned into a leopard in *Cat Girl*
☆ Lota	*Island of Lost Souls*
☆ Mayor Ben	Leopard from *Zoobiliee Zoo*
☆ Niko	Gasoline company mascot tiger
☆ Nissa	Leopard who played Baby in *Bringing Up Baby*
☆ Numa	Lion from *Tarzan*
☆ Neil	Lion from *The Bionic Woman*
☆ Nero	Lion from *Circus Boy*
☆ Raunchy	Acting jaguar
☆ Remy	"Lion girl" in *Tarzan* TV show
☆ Rigo	Gasoline company mascot tiger
☆ Rocky	Bobcat from TV commercials
☆ Sabu	Tiger from *A Tiger Walks*
☆ Sir Tom	Mountain Lion from *The Cat*
☆ Slats	One of the MGM movie studio mascot lions
☆ Tanner	One of the MGM movie studio mascot lions
☆ Satin	Tiger from *Demetrius and the Gladiators*
☆ The Amaru	Fictional jaguar spirit on *The X Files*
☆ Van Gogh	Lion from *Zoobiliee Zoo*
☆ Zamba	Lion from *The Lion*

Cat Tales

Cats can often be found not only sitting on the pages of open books, but also inhabiting the pages of closed ones. Inherently captivating, they are usually the heroes or heroines of a tale, the villains only occasionally. Peruse this list of cat character names—perhaps one of them will jump out at you.

NAME	BOOK
☐ Ariel	*The Tiger in the House*
☐ Austin	*Summon the Keeper*
☐ Ayesha	*Phantom*
☐ Basil	*Basil the Bionic Cat*
☐ Begemot	*The Master and Margarita*
☐ Big Mike	The *Big Mike* Mysteries
☐ Binky	*All I Need to Know I Learned from My Cat*
☐ Bloomburg	*Franny and Zooey*
☐ Boche	*The Diary of Anne Frank*
☐ Brobdingnagian	*Gulliver's Travels*
☐ Bubastis	*The Watchmen*
☐ Bungle	*The Patchwork Girl of Oz*
☐ Carbonel	*Carbonel: The King of the Cats*
☐ Catarina	*The Black Cat*
☐ Catasauqua	*Letters from Earth*
☐ Childebrand	*La Ménagerie Intime*
☐ Checkers	The *Jenny Linsky* Books
☐ Cheshire Cat	*Alice's Adventures in Wonderland*
☐ Cléopatrea	*La Ménagerie Intime*
☐ Crookshanks	The *Harry Potter* Books
☐ Dinah	*Alice's Adventures in Wonderland*
☐ Dikkie Dik	*Dikkie Dik*

NAME	BOOK
❑ Don Pierrot de Navarre	*La Ménagerie Intime*
❑ Dulice	The *Joe Gray* Mysteries
❑ Eatbugs	*Tailchaser's Song*
❑ Edward	The *Jenny Linsky* Books
❑ Elder Paw	The *Varjak Paw* Books
❑ Enjoras	*La Ménagerie Intime*
❑ Eponine	*La Ménagerie Intime*
❑ Eureka	*The Patchwork Girl of Oz*
❑ Feathers	*The Tiger in the House*
❑ Firsa Roofshadow	*Tailchaser's Song*
❑ Fleabag	*Fleabag and the Ring of Fire*
❑ Flyball	*Space Cat*
❑ Foss	*The Heraldic Blazon of Foss the Cat*
❑ Franchette	*Claudine at School, Claudine in Paris*
❑ Fritti Tailchaser	*Tailchaser's Song*
❑ Gareth	*Time Cat*
❑ Gavroche	*La Ménagerie Intime*
❑ Ginger	*Ginger and Pickles*
❑ Gingivere	The *Redwall* Series
❑ Gobbolino	*Gobbolino, the Witch's Cat*
❑ Graymalkin	*Macbeth*
❑ Greebo	*Discworld*
❑ Grizraz Hearteater	*Tailchaser's Song*
❑ Hamilcar	*Le Crime de Sylvestre Bonnard*
❑ Harriet	The *Catwings* Books
❑ Hamlet	*Algonquin Cat*
❑ Henrietta	*The Cat Who Covered the World*
❑ Helsa	*The Catswold Portal*
❑ Hiddigeigei	*Der Trompeter Von Säckingen*
❑ Hodge	Boswell's *Life of Johnson*
❑ Hushpad	The Catswold Portal
❑ Itty	*Dr. Doolittle's Return*
❑ James	*James, the Connoisseur Cat;* The *Catwings* Books

NAME	BOOK
❑ Jane	The *Catwings* Books
❑ Jennie Baldwin	*The Abandoned*
❑ Jenny Linsky	The *Jenny Linsky* Books
❑ Joe Gray	The *Joe Gray* Mysteries
❑ Kaid	The *Sholan Alliance* Books
❑ Karma	The *Midnight Louie* Mysteries
❑ Kiki-la-Doucette	*Sept Dialogues de Bêtes*
❑ Koko	*The Cat Who Could Read Backwards*
❑ Jalal	The *Varjak Paw* Books
❑ Kusac	The *Sholan Alliance* Books
❑ Lady Jane	*Bleak House*
❑ Leo	*Leo the Magnificent*
❑ Lionel	*The Cat Who Wished to Be a Man*
❑ Madame Théophile	*La Ménagerie Intime*
❑ Marty	*Space Cat*
❑ Maurice	*The Amazing Maurice and His Educated Rodents*
❑ McCabe	*The Catswold Portal*
❑ Mehitabel	*The Life and Times of Archy and Mehitabel*
❑ Midnight Louie	The *Midnight Louie* Mysteries
❑ Melissa	*The Catswold Portal*
❑ Minnaloushe	*The Cat and the Moon*
❑ Minon	*Prince Dorus*
❑ Mistigris	*Le Pére Goriot*
❑ Mittins	*The Tale of Samuel Whiskers*
❑ Mog	The *Mog* Series
❑ Molson	*Dr. Nightingale Meets Puss in Boots*
❑ Monsieur Tibault	*The King of Cats*
❑ Moofa	*Space Cat*
❑ Monty	*Nine Lives to Murder*
❑ Moppet	*The Story of Miss Moppet*
❑ Mrs. Moore	*The Lighthouse, the Cat, and the Sea*
❑ Ms. Jane Tabby	The *Catwings* Books
❑ Mrs. Norris	The *Harry Potter* Books
❑ Nero Corleone	*Nero Corleone: A Cat Story*

NAME	BOOK
❏ Noel	*Olga Meets Her Match*
❏ Norton	*The Cat Who Went to Paris*
❏ Orlando	*Orlando, the Marmalade Cat*
❏ Paddy	The *Mrs. Murphy* Books
❏ Pinky	*The Cat That Overcame*
❏ Percy	*The Tale of Little Pig Robinson*
❏ Peter Brown	*The Abandoned*
❏ Petronious Arbiter	*The Door Into Summer*
❏ Pewter	The *Mrs. Murphy* Books
❏ Pickles	*Pickles the Fire Cat*
❏ Picky-Picky	The *Ramona* Books
❏ Pinkle Purr	*Pinkle Purr*
❏ Pippin	*The Catswold Portal*
❏ Pixel	*The Cat Who Walked Through Walls*
❏ Polar Bear	*The Cat Who Came For Christmas*
❏ Pouncequick	*Tailchaser's Song*
❏ Puff	*Fun with Dick and Jane*
❏ Raton	*The Monkey and the Cat*
❏ Razor	The *Varjak Paw* Books
❏ Rhiow	*The Book of Night with Moon*
❏ Riggu Felis	The *Redwall* Series
❏ Roger	The *Catwings* Books
❏ Saha	*La Chatte*
❏ Sally Bones	The *Varjak Paw* Books
❏ Sam	*Broomsticks*
❏ Samson	The *Church Mice* Books

NAME	BOOK
❏ Sandigomm	The *Redwall* Series
❏ Serephita	*La Ménagerie Intime*
❏ Sherlock	*Murder at Monticello, or Old Sins*
❏ Simpkin	*Tailor of Gloucester*
❏ Singenpoo	***The Paw Thing***
❏ Sir Green Eyes	*The Dandy Cat*
❏ Slinky Malinki	*Slinky Malinki Catflaps*
❏ Snowdrop	*Alice's Adventures In Wonderland*
❏ Sootica	*Gobbolino, the Witch's Cat*
❏ Squintina	*The Tale of the Pie and the Patty-Pan*
❏ T'Chebbi	The *Sholan Alliance* Books
❏ Tabitha Twitchit	*The Tale of Tom Kitten*
❏ Tag	*The Wild Road*
❏ Tam	The *Redwall* Series
❏ Tattoo	*Pinkle Purr*
❏ Thelma	The *Catwings* Books
❏ Therma	*The Cat Who Came in From the Cold*
❏ Thomas Gray	*Thomas Gray, the Philosopher Cat*
❏ Three O'Clock Louie	The *Midnight Louie* Mysteries
❏ Tibert	*Reynard the Fox*
❏ Timorell	*The Catswold Portal*
❏ Tobermorey	*The Chronicles of Clovis*
❏ Tom Quartz	*Roughing It*
❏ Trim	*Trim*
❏ Tsarmina	The *Redwall* Series
❏ Verdauga Greeneyes	The *Redwall* Series
❏ Ungatt Trunn	The *Redwall* Series
❏ Varjak Paw	The *Varjak Paw* Books
❏ Webster	*The Story of Webster*
❏ White Noise	*The Happy Hollisters*
❏ William	*The Cat in the Lifeboat*

NAME	BOOK
☐ Wolsey	*The New Adventures of Doctor Who*
☐ Yvette	The *Midnight Louie* Mysteries
☐ Zainal	The *Freedom* Trilogy
☐ Zapaquilda	*The Battle of the Cats*
☐ Zizi	*La Ménagerie Intime*
☐ Zoom	*Zoom at Sea*

Practical Cat Names

T.S. Eliot—poet, Nobel Prize winner, Cat Namer Extraordinaire. Sure, *The Love Song of J. Alfred Prufrock* is an enduring statement on the human condition, but for cat names, you can't do better than Eliot's *Old Possum's Book of Practical Cats*. The book, which inspired the musical *Cats*, is (pardon the pun) littered with dozens of creative cat names, one of which might be just the one you're looking for.

☆ Admetus
☆ Alonzo
☆ Augustus
☆ Bill Baily
☆ Bombalurina
☆ Bustopher Jones
☆ Cat Morgan
☆ Coricopat
☆ Demeter
☆ Electra
☆ George
☆ Gilbert
☆ Griddlebone
☆ Growltiger

☆ Grumbuskin
☆ Gus
　(aka Asparagus)
☆ James
☆ Jellylorum
☆ Jennyanydots
☆ Jonathan
☆ Macavity
☆ Mr. Mistoffelees
☆ Mungojerrie
☆ Munkustrap
☆ Old Deuteronomy
☆ Old Gumbie Cat
☆ Oopsa Cat
　(aka James Buz-James)

☆ Peter
☆ Plato
☆ Quaxo
☆ Rumpelteazer
☆ Skimbleshanks
☆ The Great Rumpus Cat
☆ The Rum Tum Tugger
☆ Tumblebrutus
☆ Victor

Cari-Cat-Ures

Cartoons, comics, and cats go together. On the big screen and the little screen, in the newspaper or on a computer screen, cats have inspired many an artist and animator. Does your cat call to mind the heavy-lidded irony of GARFIELD? The cool confidence of the strays in THE ARISTICATS? The tactical genius of a video game cat? With a name from one of these lists, your cat can follow in the paw prints of some of the most memorable cats in many media.

Comic Cats

Some are slapstick, some are droll, but they've all got great names. Check out this list of comic cats for some really original ideas.

CAT	COMIC
❏ Apathy Kat	*Apathy Kat*
❏ Arlene	*Garfield*
❏ Attila	*Mother Goose and Grimm*
❏ Bill the Cat	*Bloom County* cartoons
❏ Bella	*Beetle Bailey*
❏ Bête Noir	*Gordo*
❏ Bucky Katt	*Get Fuzzy*
❏ Boom Boom Pussini	*Heathcliff*
❏ Captain Amerikat	*Marvel Tails*
❏ Catbert	*Dilbert*
❏ Cat Jacob	*Cat Jacob*
❏ Choo Choo Bear	*Something Positive*
❏ Chubby Huggs	*Get Fuzzy*
❏ Curly	*Garfield's Nine Lives*
❏ Dinky	*Felix the Cat*
❏ Desdemona	*Matt and Jeff*
❏ Dr. Video	*Kelly and Duke*
❏ Ele	*Non Sequitur*
❏ Esmeralda	*Cicero's Cat*
❏ Faron	*Peanuts*
❏ Fleshy	*Monty*
❏ Fluffy	*Darkwing Duck*
❏ Fritz	*Fritz the Cat*
❏ Gatita	*Krazy Kat*

CAT	COMIC
❏ Heathcliff	*Heathcliff*
❏ Hope	*The Gumps*
❏ Horse	*Footrot Flats*
❏ Hot Dog	*Dennis the Menace*
❏ Icky	*Felix the Cat*
❏ King Kat	*King Kat*
❏ Krazy Kat	*Krazy Kat*
❏ Moe	*Garfield*
❏ Mootchie	*Mutts*
❏ Mr. MeeYowl	*Krazy Kat*
❏ Mr. Noodles	*Mutts*
❏ Nelly	*Mutts*
❏ Nermal	*Garfield*
❏ Old Eli	*Garfield*
❏ Ollie	*Ollie the Alley Cat*
❏ PeekaBoo	*Rose is Rose*
❏ Penny	*Stray Cats*
❏ Pixel	*PC and Pixel*
❏ Pussy Gato	*Gordo*
❏ Pussycat Princess	*Pussycat Princess*
❏ Schtinky	*Mutts*
❏ Shnelly	*Mutts*
❏ Shnooky	*Mutts*
❏ Spooky	*Spooky*
❏ Streaky the Supercat	*Supergirl*
❏ Sumo	*Mother Goose and Grimm*
❏ Suppi	*Cardcaptor Sakura*
❏ Tabbe Le Fauve	*Xanadu*
❏ Tish	*Mutts*
❏ Twisp	*Penny Arcade*

CAT	COMIC
☐ Wannyan	*UFO Baby*
☐ Winson	*Bash Street Kids*
☐ Wuggums	*Bloom County*
☐ WW II	*Peanuts*

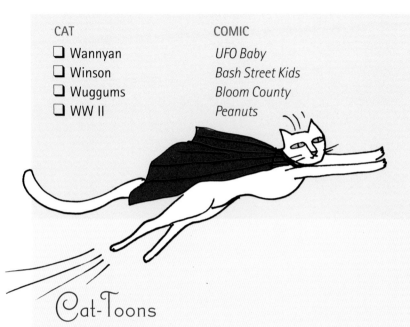

Cat-Toons

They talk, they dance, they save the world. These cartoon kitties are great role models for your own little wonder cat.

CAT	SHOW
☐ Abby the Olympic Tabby	*The Simpsons*
☐ Alley-Kat-Abra	*Teen Titans*
☐ Annabelle	*Eeek! The Cat*
☐ Ann Gora	*SWAT Kats*
☐ Artemis	*Sailor Moon*
☐ Autocat	*The Cattanooga Cats; Autocat and Motormouse*
☐ Azrael	*The Smurfs*
☐ Baba Miao	*Sagwa, The Chinese Siamese Cat*
☐ Babbit	*Looney Toons*

CAT	SHOW
☐ Baby Puss	*The Flintstones*
☐ Baby Sylvester	*Looney Toons*
☐ Bat Cat	*Samauri Pizza Cat*
☐ Baggypants	*Baggypants and Friends*
☐ Baudelaire	*Phantom 2040*
☐ Benny the Ball	*Top Cat*
☐ Binka	*Binka the Cat*
☐ Blue Kitty	*Voltron*
☐ Bonkers	*Bonkers*
☐ Boo	*Funky Phantom*
☐ Bowser	*Mr. Magoo*
☐ Brain	*Top Cat*
☐ Brassel	*SWAT Kats*
☐ Burke	*SWAT Kats*
☐ Cagney	*Gargoyles*
☐ Callie Briggs	*SWAT Kats*
☐ Catastrophe	*SpyDogs*
☐ Catgut	*Pound Puppies*
☐ Catstello	*Looney Toons*
☐ Chance Furlong	*SWAT Kats*
☐ Charlemange	*Anatole*
☐ Chessie	*The Cattanooga Cats*
☐ Chip	*Phish and Chip*
	What-A-Cartoon Show
☐ Claude Cat	*Looney Tunes*
☐ Clean Cat	*Yogi's Space Race*
☐ Cleo	*Heathcliff*
☐ Choo Choo	*Top Cat*
☐ Coltrane	*The Simpsons*
☐ Commander Ulysses Feral	*SWAT Kats*
☐ Country	*The Cattanooga Cats*

CAT	SHOW
❏ Courageous Cat	*Courageous Cat and Minute Mouse*
❏ Crazy Shirley	*Heathcliff*
❏ Custard	*Strawberry Shortcake*
❏ Dark Kat	*SWAT Kats*
❏ David Litterbin	*SWAT Kats*
❏ Diana	*Sailor Moon*
❏ Dongwa	*Sagwa, The Chinese Siamese Cat*
❏ Doraemon	*Doraemon*
❏ Dr. Abi Sinian	*SWAT Kats*
❏ Dr. Leiter Greenbox	*SWAT Kats*
❏ Dr. Viper	*SWAT Kats*
❏ Dr. Zyme	*SWAT Kats*
❏ Eek	*Eek! The Cat*
❏ Fancy	*Top Cat*
❏ Fat Cat	*Chip 'n Dale Rescue Rangers*
❏ Felix	*Felix the Cat*
❏ Felina Feral	*SWAT Kats*
❏ Felina Furr	*Teen Titans*
❏ Fifi	*Looney Toons*
❏ Francine	*Samurai Pizza Cats*
❏ Furball	*Tiny Toons*
❏ Goldie	*Top Cat*
❏ Groovy	*The Cattanooga Cats*
❏ Guido Anchovy	*Samurai Pizza Cats*
❏ Hard Drive	*SWAT Kats*
❏ Hector	*Heathcliff*
❏ Hogan the Wonder Cat	*Samurai Pizza Cats*
❏ Igor	*The World's Greatest Superfriends*
❏ Isis	*Batman*

CAT	SHOW
☐ Jake Clawson	*SWAT Kats*
☐ Jenji	*Power Rangers: Mystic Force*
☐ Jenny	*Bucky O'Hare*
☐ Jingoro	*Kimagure Orange Road*
☐ Johnny K	*SWAT Kats*
☐ Kahti	*Mummies Alive*
☐ Katnip	*Herman and Katnip/The Baby Huey Show*
☐ Kitty	*Powerpuff Girls*
☐ Kitty Jo	*The Cattanooga Cats*
☐ Klondike Kat	*Underdog*
☐ Lenny Ringtail	*SWAT Kats*
☐ Luna	*Sailor Moon*
☐ Mac Mange	*SWAT Kats*
☐ Madame Nietzsche	*The Mouse and the Monster*
☐ MadKat	*SWAT Kats*
☐ Mama Miao	*Sagwa, the Chinese Siamese Cat*
☐ Mayor Manx	*SWAT Kats*
☐ Meowzma	*Samurai Pizza Cats*
☐ Mittens	*The Simpsons*
☐ Molly Mange	*SWAT Kats*

CAT	SHOW
❏ Mr. Chubbikins	*Freakazoid*
❏ Mr. Kitty	*South Park*
❏ Mr. Meow	*Mr. Meow*
❏ Mr. Snookums	*The Simpsons*
❏ Mungo	*Heathcliff*
❏ Murray	*SWAT Kats*
❏ Mutilor	*SWAT Kats*
❏ Nataska Slinky	*The Twisted Tales of Felix the Cat*
❏ Nai-Nai	*Sagwa, the Chinese Siamese Cat*
❏ Nefertina	*Mummies Alive*
❏ P.C	*Power Rangers*
❏ Pastmaster	*SWAT Kats*
❏ Pepito	*The Simpsons*
❏ Persian Puss	*Peter and Persian*
❏ Polly Esther	*Samurai Pizza Cats*
❏ Prince Myshkin	*Noir*
❏ Professor Hackle	*SWAT Kats*
❏ Proud Heart Cat	*Care Bears*
❏ Punkin' Puss	*Punkin' Puss and Mushmouse*
❏ Pussyfoot	*Looney Toons*
❏ Razor	*SWAT Kats*
❏ Red Lynx	*SWAT Kats*
❏ Reddy	*Ruff and Reddy*
❏ Riff Raff	*Underdog*
❏ Rita	*Animaniacs*
❏ Roscoe	*The Twisted Tales of Felix the Cat*
❏ Sagwa	*Sagwa, the Chinese Siamese Cat*
❏ Scaredy Kat	*SWAT Kats*
❏ Scrapper	*Mr. Bean*
❏ Scratch	*The Biskitts*
❏ Scratchy	*The Simpsons*
❏ Scoots	*The Cattanooga Cats*

CAT	SHOW
❑ Sebastian	*Josie and the Pussycats*
❑ Shampoo	*Ranma ½*
❑ Sheegwa	*Sagwa The Chinese Siamese Cat*
❑ Sludge	*Yogi's Space Race*
❑ Snarf	*Thundercats*
❑ Snooper	*Snooper and Blooper*
❑ Snowball	*The Simpsons*
❑ Sonia	*Heathcliff*
❑ Speedy Ceriche	*Samurai Pizza Cats*
❑ Spiffy	*The Oddball Couple*
❑ Spook	*Top Cat*
❑ Spot	*Hong Kong Phooey*
❑ Spritz the Cat	*Samurai Pizza Cats*
❑ Steele	*SWAT Kats*
❑ Stimpson J. Cat	*The Ren and Stimpy Show*
❑ Sylvester T. Pussycat	*Looney Toons*
❑ T-Bone	*SWAT Kats*
❑ Tabor	*SWAT Kats*
❑ Tamala	*Tamala 2010: Punk Cat in Space*
❑ Tiger Conklin	*SWAT Kats*
❑ Tom	*Tom and Jerry*
❑ Top Cat	*Top Cat*
❑ Turmoil	*SWAT Kats*
❑ Waffles	*The Goof Troop*
❑ Whiskers	*Whiskers, the Cat Who Can Name Fruit*
❑ Wordsworth	*Heathcliff*
❑ Yeh-Yeh	*Sagwa, the Chinese Siamese Cat*
❑ ZaZa	*Hector's House*

Cat Hollywood

Some animated cats have hit the big time.

CAT	MOVIE
☐ Am	*Lady and the Tramp*
☐ Baron	*The Cat Returns*
☐ Berlioz	*The Aristocats*
☐ Billy Bass	*The Aristocats*
☐ Captain Amelia	*Treasure Planet*
☐ Catbus	*My Neighbor Totoro*
☐ Cat R. Waul	*An American Tale: Fieval Goes West*
☐ Cheshire Cat	*Alice in Wonderland*
☐ Danny	*Cats Don't Dance*
☐ Darla Dimple	*Cats Don't Dance*
☐ Duchess	*The Aristocats*
☐ Figaro	*Pinocchio*

CAT	MOVIE
❑ Hit Cat	*The Aristocats*
❑ Jaune-Tom	*Gay Puree*
❑ Lucifer	*Cinderella*
❑ Marie	*The Aristocats*
❑ Meowrice	*Gay Puree*
❑ Oliver	*Oliver and Company*
❑ O'Malley	*The Aristocats*
❑ P.J.	*A Goofy Movie*
❑ Peppo	*The Aristocats*
❑ Pete	*A Goofy Movie*
❑ Puss In Boots	*Shrek*
❑ Robespierre	*Gay Puree*
❑ Rufus	*The Rescuers*
❑ Sawyer	*Cats Don't Dance*
❑ Scat Cat	*The Aristocats*
❑ Sergeant Tibbs	*101 Dalmatians*
❑ Shun Gon	*The Aristocats*
❑ Si	*Lady and the Tramp*
❑ Tiger	*An American Tale: Fieval Goes West*
❑ Toulouse	*The Aristocats*

The Biggest Cats

Larger than life, and larger than house cats, these movie
and TV felines (and their names) make a big impression.

NAME	SPECIES	SHOW
☆ Anastasia	Tiger	*The Simpsons*
☆ Annie	Girl/Panther	*Rainbow Panthers*
☆ Bagheera	Panther	*The Jungle Book*
☆ Battle Cat	Tiger	*Masters of the Universe*
☆ Brave Heart	Lion	*The Care Bears*
☆ Cheetara	Girl/Cheetah	*Thundercats*
☆ Goliath	Dog/Lion	*Young Samson*
☆ Howl	Lion	*Rainbow Panthers*
☆ Janguru Taitei	Lion	*Kimba the White Lion*
☆ Kiara	Lion	*Lion King II*
☆ Kimba	Lion	*Kimba the White Lion*
☆ Kovu	Lion	*Lion King II*
☆ Leo	Lion	*Kimba the White Lion*
☆ Lion-O	Boy/Lion	*Thundercats*
☆ Mufasa	Lion	*The Lion King*
☆ Nala	Lion	*The Lion King*
☆ Panky	Panther	*Rainbow Panthers*
☆ Pink Panther	Panther	*The Pink Panther*
☆ Panthro	Panther	*Rainbow Panthers*
☆ Pinky	Panther	*Rainbow Panthers*
☆ Punkin	Panther	*Rainbow Panthers*
☆ Priscilla Rica	Cheetah	*Challenge of the Superheroes*
☆ Rags	Tiger	*Crusader Rabbit*
☆ Rajah	Tiger	*Aladdin*
☆ Rocko	Panther	*Rainbow Panthers*
☆ Scar	Lion	*The Lion King*
☆ Serabe	Lion	*The Lion King*
☆ Shere Khan	Tiger	*The Jungle Book*
☆ Simba	Lion	*The Lion King*
☆ Tygra	Tiger	*Thundercats*
☆ Wiley Catt	Wildcat	*Pogo*
☆ Wilykat	Wildcat	*Thundercats*
☆ Wilykit	Wildcat	*Thundercats*
☆ Zira	Lion	*Lion King II*

Game Cats

Does your cat have certain super powers that defy logical explanation? Perhaps a video game cat name would make sense for her.

NAME	GAME
❑ Alfador	*Chrono Trigger*
❑ Amazoness Tiger	*Yu-Gi-Oh*
❑ Big the Cat	*Sonic Adventure*
❑ Blaze the Cat	*Sonic Rush*
❑ Blinx	*Blinx: The Time Sweeper*
❑ Cait Sith	*Final Fantasy VII*
❑ Catnipped Kitty	*Yu-Gi-Oh*
❑ Captain Nathaniel Claw	*Claw*
❑ CatBat	*Wario Land 4*
❑ Cray	*Breath of Fire*
❑ Delcatty	*Pokémon*
❑ Elsie	*Stanley*
❑ Espeon	*Pokémon*
❑ Evil the Cat	*Earthworm Jim*
❑ Faustus	*Captain Atom*
❑ Fusionist	*Yu-Gi-Oh*
❑ Glameow	*Pokémon*
❑ Hershey	*Sonic Hedgehog*
❑ Juliette	*Fur Fighters*
❑ Juhani	*Star Wars: Knights of the Republic*
❑ Katt	*Breath of Fire*
❑ Leogun	*Yu-Gi-Oh*
❑ Katt Monroe	*Star Fox 64/Lylat Wars*
❑ Kay	*Legend of Kay*

NAME	GAME
❏ King Tiger Wanghu	*Yu-Gi-Oh*
❏ Lady Panther	*Yu-Gi-Oh*
❏ Little Chimera	*Yu-Gi-Oh*
❏ Lin	*Breath of Fire*
❏ Luxio	*Pokémon*
❏ luxray	*Pokémon*
❏ Meowth	*Pokémon*
❏ Mew	*Pokémon*
❏ Mewtwo	*Pokémon*
❏ Mithra	*Final Fantasy IV*
❏ Musk Cat	*Phantasy Star*
❏ Muu	*Pokémon*
❏ Neko Mane King	*Yu-Gi-Oh*
❏ Nifta	*Wizball*
❏ Panther Warrior	*Yu-Gi-Oh*
❏ Persian	*Pokémon*
❏ Purugly	*Pokémon*
❏ Red VIII	*Final Fantasy VII*
❏ Rei	*Breath of Fire*
❏ Rescue Cat	*Yu-Gi-Oh*
❏ Shinx	*Pokémon*
❏ Skitty	*Pokémon*
❏ Sleeping Lion	*Yu-Gi-Oh*
❏ Strudel	*Time Splitters*
❏ Soul Tiger	*Yu-Gi-Oh*
❏ Sourpuss	*Pac Man*
❏ Spitz	*Warioware*
❏ Tango	*Mega Man V/Rockman World 5*
❏ Tat	*Klonoa 2: Lunatea's Veil*
❏ Tiga	*Breath of Fire 2*
❏ Tiger Axe	*Yu-Gi-Oh*
❏ Turtle Tiger	*Yu-Gi-Oh*
❏ Zombie Tiger	*Yu-Gi-Oh*

Kitty City

Certain cats have that look that brings to mind exotic locales—tropical islands or faraway romantic cities. If your own life leaves you too busy to get away, you can always live vicariously through your favorite feline. Paris, Tahiti, Malibu—they're just a "catcall" away.

- Abaco
- Adelaide
- Andalusia
- Andorra
- Antigua
- Aruba
- Astoria
- Azores
- Babylon
- Bali
- Baja
- Bermuda
- Bikini
- Boca
- Boise
- Broadway
- Brooklyn
- Cádiz
- Calais
- Caicos
- Carolina
- Carmel
- Casbah
- Catalina
- Cayman
- Cluny
- Cordoba
- Corfu
- Cortez
- Cuba
- Curacao
- Dallas
- Danube
- Delhi
- Dixie
- Dominica
- Fez
- Firenze
- Fiji
- Fuji
- Frisco
- Geneva
- Georgia
- Grenada
- Halifax
- Hollywood
- India
- Jamaica
- Jersey
- Kenya
- Kerala
- Kiev
- Kittery
- Kona
- Kyoto
- Lamu
- La Paz
- Laramie
- Laredo
- Lhasa
- Palmyra
- Panama
- Principé

- ❏ Malmo
- ❏ Malabar
- ❏ Malibu
- ❏ Martinique
- ❏ Maui
- ❏ Milan
- ❏ Moloka'i
- ❏ Monterrey
- ❏ Montserrat
- ❏ Mumbai
- ❏ Mustique
- ❏ Napa
- ❏ Niagara
- ❏ Oaxaca
- ❏ Odessa
- ❏ Oahu
- ❏ Orlando
- ❏ Oslo
- ❏ Paris
- ❏ Phuket
- ❏ Reno
- ❏ Rio
- ❏ Roma
- ❏ Saba

- ❏ St. Kitts
- ❏ Saipan
- ❏ Samoa
- ❏ Santiago
- ❏ Savannah
- ❏ Sedona
- ❏ Seychelles
- ❏ Siena
- ❏ Sonora
- ❏ Sydney
- ❏ Taos
- ❏ Tahiti
- ❏ Tahoe
- ❏ Tenerife
- ❏ Tex
- ❏ Thames
- ❏ Tijuana
- ❏ Timbuktu
- ❏ Toulouse
- ❏ Tulsa
- ❏ Surrey
- ❏ Vegas
- ❏ Vienna
- ❏ Zanzibar

A Different Breed of Cat

With their impeccable breeding and predictable temperaments, pedigreed pusses are, some would say, the cat's pajamas. There are more than 100 recognized breeds: here are 14 of the most popular, and some distinctive names for each.

Abyssinian

Modern-day Ethiopia was the ancient kingdom of Abyssinia. These names come from the people and places of that historic region.

- ❏ Abba
- ❏ Abebe
- ❏ Abeba
- ❏ Adina
- ❏ Adwa
- ❏ Adi
- ❏ Asmara
- ❏ Azmera
- ❏ Dawit
- ❏ Desta
- ❏ Dinka
- ❏ Dinku
- ❏ Ephraim
- ❏ Furgassa
- ❏ Haile-Selassie
- ❏ Haj
- ❏ Hakim
- ❏ Iksandar
- ❏ Kassa
- ❏ Makeda
- ❏ Melesse
- ❏ Saba

- ❏ Samson
- ❏ Sossina
- ❏ Selassie
- ❏ Shebelle
- ❏ Tabi
- ❏ Tefere
- ❏ Tekle
- ❏ Tigray
- ❏ Tigre
- ❏ Tigrinya
- ❏ Zen
- ❏ Zenia
- ❏ Zula

Australian Mist

G'day, kitty. Try one of these Australia-inspired names for your Misty.

- ❏ Adelaide
- ❏ Aussie
- ❏ Barbie
- ❏ Billabong
- ❏ Boomerang
- ❏ Bushie
- ❏ Didgeridoo
- ❏ Dinkum
- ❏ Dinki-di

Balinese

Balinese naming traditions are a bit complicated, but these selections, based on the locales and inhabitants of the beautiful Indonesian island, are a good place to start.

- ❏ Dundee
- ❏ Dreamtime
- ❏ Emu
- ❏ Jackaroo
- ❏ Jillaroo
- ❏ Kanga
- ❏ Koala
- ❏ Marmite
- ❏ Matilda
- ❏ Mate
- ❏ Sheila
- ❏ Sydney
- ❏ Wallaby
- ❏ Wallaroo
- ❏ Wombat

- ❏ Bagus
- ❏ Batik
- ❏ Batur
- ❏ Candi Dasa
- ❏ Catur
- ❏ Dayu
- ❏ Dewa
- ❏ Dewi
- ❏ Gede
- ❏ Gitgit
- ❏ Kadek
- ❏ Ketut
- ❏ Lovina
- ❏ Kintamani
- ❏ Komang
- ❏ Kuta

- ❏ Nusa Dua
- ❏ Raka
- ❏ Rai
- ❏ Pasut
- ❏ Putu
- ❏ Rubaya
- ❏ Sanur
- ❏ Sawan
- ❏ Segara
- ❏ Singaraja
- ❏ Soka
- ❏ Surya
- ❏ Tembok
- ❏ Tuban
- ❏ Ulu Watu
- ❏ Wayan

Birman and Burmese

Birman and Burmese cats originate from the area now known as Myanmar, once known as Mandalay. A name from this list—some from English and Portuguese colonists and some traditional—might enhance your cat's exotic appeal.

- ☐ Arakan
- ☐ Chin
- ☐ Chit
- ☐ Cho
- ☐ Dhaka
- ☐ Kachin
- ☐ Mandalay
- ☐ Maymyo
- ☐ Mya
- ☐ Myanmar
- ☐ Nanda
- ☐ Rangoon
- ☐ Sandi
- ☐ Sandoway
- ☐ Than
- ☐ Zeya

British Longhair

Long live the Longhair. These very names call to mind the storied traditions of the British Isles.

- ☐ Chester
- ☐ Catswold
  (play on Cotswolds)
- ☐ Cricket
- ☐ Elizabeth
- ☐ Eton
- ☐ Guinevere
- ☐ Hamish
- ☐ Harrod
- ☐ Hippie
- ☐ Henley

Cornish Rex

Cornwall's distinctive language and history gave rise to such delightful place names as Puddle, Padstow, and Old Grimsby. Good luck picking just one.

- [ ] Baldy
- [ ] Brighton
- [ ] Crumplehorn
- [ ] Dizzard
- [ ] Falmouth
- [ ] Freathy

- [ ] Gwills
- [ ] Hugus
- [ ] Jolly Bottom
- [ ] Joppa
- [ ] Kernow
- [ ] Mawla

- [ ] Maxworthy
- [ ] Mingoose
- [ ] Morval
- [ ] Mousehole
- [ ] Old Grimsby
- [ ] Padstow
- [ ] Pasty
- [ ] Pennytinney
- [ ] Penzance
- [ ] Puddle
- [ ] Readymoney
- [ ] Regina
- [ ] Rex
- [ ] Salem
- [ ] Skewes
- [ ] Stargazey
- [ ] Stibb
- [ ] Sticker
- [ ] St. Blazey
- [ ] St. Ives
- [ ] Talskiddy
- [ ] Tamar
- [ ] Tomperrow
- [ ] Tutwell
- [ ] Viscar
- [ ] Wooley
- [ ] Woon

- [ ] Kipling
- [ ] Lancelot
- [ ] Lionheart
- [ ] Maid Marian
- [ ] Mersey
- [ ] Monty
- [ ] Nelson
- [ ] Nigel
- [ ] Nigella
- [ ] Piccadilly
- [ ] Pip
- [ ] Poppy
- [ ] Posh
- [ ] Professor Longhair

- [ ] Pudding
- [ ] Pym
- [ ] Quid
- [ ] Snooker
- [ ] Tavistock
- [ ] Thames
- [ ] Torquay
- [ ] Tuppence
- [ ] Victoria
- [ ] Wembley
- [ ] Wimbledon
- [ ] Windsor

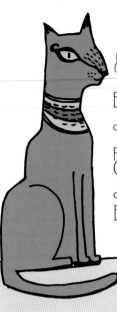

Egyptian Mau

Egypt is considered the spiritual home of cats around the world. From the pyramids at Giza to the busy streets of Cairo, cats play a big part in Egyptian culture. Why not choose one of these Egyptian names of note?

- ❑ Akil
- ❑ Ako
- ❑ Amenhotep
- ❑ Anwar
- ❑ Aswan
- ❑ Azizi
- ❑ Bakara
- ❑ Cairo
- ❑ Bubu
- ❑ Cleopatra
- ❑ Femi
- ❑ Gizeh
- ❑ Hatshepsut
- ❑ Hasina
- ❑ Hebony
- ❑ Hondo
- ❑ Isis
- ❑ Jafari
- ❑ Kebi
- ❑ Kesi
- ❑ Khait
- ❑ Kifi
- ❑ Kissa
- ❑ Kiya
- ❑ Layla
- ❑ Luxor
- ❑ Mandisa
- ❑ Mesi
- ❑ Miu
- ❑ Miw-Sher
- ❑ Monifa
- ❑ Nassar
- ❑ Nefertiti
- ❑ Nuri
- ❑ Omari
- ❑ Osiris
- ❑ Pharaoh
- ❑ Qeb
- ❑ Ramses
- ❑ Rashida
- ❑ Sabah
- ❑ Set
- ❑ Seth
- ❑ Siti
- ❑ Suez
- ❑ Tabia
- ❑ Thutmose
- ❑ Tut
- ❑ Wati
- ❑ Zuberi

Manx

Situated in the Irish Sea, The Isle of Man has a distinctive flavor that blends English, Scottish, and Irish culture. Doesn't your Manx deserve a name as unique as he is?

☐ Aelid
☐ Aimel
☐ Ailesreena
☐ Alistar
☐ Bertram
☐ Caly
☐ Cabry
☐ Catreena
☐ Catreeney
☐ Cissolt
☐ Colum
☐ Coonie
☐ Darraty
☐ Doolish
☐ Doona
☐ Ewan
☐ Flaxney
☐ Finlo
☐ Fritha

☐ Gawain
☐ Gillo
☐ Grayse
☐ Greeba
☐ Hommy
☐ Jezabel
☐ Jinn
☐ Lallie
☐ Laurys
☐ Mappy
☐ Markys
☐ Moggy
☐ Moiree
☐ Nessy
☐ Padeen
☐ Stoill
☐ Sorcha
☐ Tosha
☐ Una

Maine Coon

Consider one of these Maine-inspired names for your "gentle giant."

- ☐ Allagash
- ☐ Alna
- ☐ Amity
- ☐ Bangor
- ☐ Bean (L.L.)
- ☐ Berwick
- ☐ Biddeford
- ☐ Blueberry
- ☐ Bowdoin
- ☐ Calais
- ☐ Caribou
- ☐ Casco
- ☐ Chester
- ☐ Chelsea
- ☐ China
- ☐ Cooper
- ☐ Corinna
- ☐ Eliot
- ☐ Gilead
- ☐ Hiram
- ☐ Hollis
- ☐ Kennebec
- ☐ Kittery
- ☐ Mechias
- ☐ Meddybemps
- ☐ Mexico
- ☐ Milo
- ☐ Minot
- ☐ Millinocket
- ☐ Monson
- ☐ Palmyra
- ☐ Paris
- ☐ Penobscot
- ☐ Patten
- ☐ Rangeley
- ☐ Ripley
- ☐ Sabbatus
- ☐ Saco
- ☐ Sebago
- ☐ Shirley
- ☐ Troy
- ☐ Veazie
- ☐ Waldo

Norwegian Forest Cat

One of the few cats from the North, the Norwegian Forest Cat is a hardy soul who loves the great outdoors. Honor your WEIGE'S Scandinavian heritage with a winner from this list.

- ☐ Alf
- ☐ Astra
- ☐ Astrid
- ☐ Balder
- ☐ Bergit
- ☐ Björn
- ☐ Canute
- ☐ Catrine
- ☐ Dag

Persian

Possibly the first, and arguably the most distinguished, breed, the Persian originates from the "cradle of civilization." Choose an epic name for your epic kitty.

- ❑ Dagmar
- ❑ Danica
- ❑ Emil
- ❑ Freya
- ❑ Fricka
- ❑ Gerda
- ❑ Gudren
- ❑ Gunnar
- ❑ Hedda
- ❑ Henriette
- ❑ Inga
- ❑ Ivar
- ❑ Lars
- ❑ Leif
- ❑ Liv
- ❑ Mads
- ❑ Magnus
- ❑ Marit
- ❑ Mikkel
- ❑ Nils
- ❑ Oslo
- ❑ Otta
- ❑ Pernilla
- ❑ Saga
- ❑ Ski
- ❑ Skog
- ❑ Skau
- ❑ Skaukatt
- ❑ Svend
- ❑ Telemark
- ❑ Tobias
- ❑ Tor
- ❑ Weige

- ❑ Amir
- ❑ Anoosheh
- ❑ Arad
- ❑ Arash
- ❑ Arsalan
- ❑ Asad
- ❑ Ava
- ❑ Azita
- ❑ Azar
- ❑ Bahar
- ❑ Banou
- ❑ Behrooz
- ❑ Bijan
- ❑ Bita
- ❑ Bousseh

- ❑ Cyras
- ❑ Danush
- ❑ Faraz
- ❑ Fareed
- ❑ Farva
- ❑ Fila
- ❑ Firouz
- ❑ Ghodsi
- ❑ Gita
- ❑ Habib
- ❑ Hassan
- ❑ Jafar
- ❑ Jalal
- ❑ Kareem
- ❑ Laleh
- ❑ Lelia
- ❑ Mahnoosh
- ❑ Mahmood
- ❑ Mansoor
- ❑ Mina
- ❑ Minoo
- ❑ Nava

- ❑ Nazilla
- ❑ Nikoo
- ❑ Noor
- ❑ Pari
- ❑ Pooneh
- ❑ Pouya
- ❑ Reza
- ❑ Roxana
- ❑ Saeed
- ❑ Salma
- ❑ Salman
- ❑ Scheherazade
- ❑ Soraya
- ❑ Suri
- ❑ Tala
- ❑ Zahra
- ❑ Zari

Scottish Fold

How about a Scottish name for your wee kit?

- ❏ Argyle
- ❏ Angus
- ❏ Bonnie
- ❏ Bruce
- ❏ Burns
- ❏ Dewar
- ❏ Duff
- ❏ Duncan
- ❏ Dumfrie
- ❏ Dundee
- ❏ Haggis
- ❏ Heather
- ❏ Highlander
- ❏ Hume
- ❏ Kiltie
- ❏ Lachlan
- ❏ MacIntosh
- ❏ McDougal
- ❏ McDuff
- ❏ McGregor
- ❏ McKenzie
- ❏ Nessie
- ❏ Orkney
- ❏ Plaid
- ❏ Stewart
- ❏ Tam O' Shanter
- ❏ Tartan

Siamese

Alluring and exotic, Siamese cats are in a class by themselves. Choose an equally exotic name from this list of place and people names from Thailand (formerly the kingdom of Siam).

- ❏ Arun
- ❏ Areya
- ❏ Chatchai
- ❏ Chiang Mai
- ❏ Erawan
- ❏ Krabi
- ❏ Malai
- ❏ Mom Chao
- ❏ Mom Luang
- ❏ Pakpao
- ❏ Pattaya
- ❏ Phi Phi
- ❏ Phuket
- ❏ Pim
- ❏ Pongrit
- ❏ Rama
- ❏ Somluck
- ❏ Somsong
- ❏ Sunya
- ❏ Sunisa
- ❏ Surat
- ❏ Surin
- ❏ Suttipong
- ❏ Taksin the Great
- ❏ Tuksin
- ❏ Yada
- ❏ Yanisa

Turkish Angora

Turkey is at the crossroads of Europe and Asia, and Turkish Angoras blend the best of both continents. You couldn't do better than one of these names for your Tur-kat.

- ❏ Adana
- ❏ Ahmet
- ❏ Ankara
- ❏ Antalya
- ❏ Aslan
- ❏ Ata
- ❏ Aydin
- ❏ Ayla
- ❏ Aysu
- ❏ Aziz
- ❏ Basri
- ❏ Burak
- ❏ Erol
- ❏ Esma
- ❏ Faruk
- ❏ Fatma
- ❏ Hakan
- ❏ Hasan
- ❏ Izmir
- ❏ Jemal
- ❏ Kahil
- ❏ Kutsi
- ❏ Levant
- ❏ Murat
- ❏ Musa
- ❏ Mustafa
- ❏ Nisa
- ❏ Ozan
- ❏ Rana
- ❏ Sema
- ❏ Serap
- ❏ Suleyman
- ❏ Tokat
- ❏ Tuba
- ❏ Vadim
- ❏ Zaide
- ❏ Zenyep

A Cat By Any Other Name

How do you say cat? Here are some examples from other languages:

NAME	LANGUAGE
☆ Besseh	Arabic
☆ Catua	Basque
☆ Chat	French
☆ Chatul	Yiddish
☆ Gato	Spanish and Portuguese
☆ Gatto	Italian
☆ Kat	Dutch and Danish
☆ Katze	German

NAME	LANGUAGE
☆ Kissa	Finnish
☆ Kočka	Czech
☆ Koshka	Russian
☆ Mah-oh	Thai
☆ Macska	Hungarian
☆ Miu	Chinese
☆ Neko	Japanese
☆ Paka	Swahili
☆ Pisică	Romanian
☆ Popoki	Hawaiian

Hep Cats

They don't call 'em cool cats for nothing. Cats INVENTED attitude. The way they move, the way they act: they're always the coolest creatures in any room. As the song says, EVERYBODY WANTS TO BE A CAT. It can be tough finding just one name that captures the essence of your cat's inner hipster, but here are some to start with. They're cool, like jazz, like the swish swish swish of a cat's tail....yeah.

The Kitties

- ☐ Aliyah
- ☐ Aja
- ☐ Ajani
- ☐ Althea
- ☐ Amani
- ☐ Anais
- ☐ Aretha
- ☐ Artemisia
- ☐ Ashanti
- ☐ Asia
- ☐ Bathsheba
- ☐ Bella
- ☐ Bindi
- ☐ Calypso
- ☐ Circe
- ☐ Citron
- ☐ Clio
- ☐ Deja
- ☐ Diva
- ☐ Dolce
- ☐ Dulce
- ☐ Ebony
- ☐ Eden
- ☐ Electra
- ☐ Eliza
- ☐ Esperanza
- ☐ Ianthe
- ☐ Jamais
- ☐ Jazz
- ☐ Josie
- ☐ Layla
- ☐ Latifah
- ☐ Lotus
- ☐ Lyric
- ☐ Maya
- ☐ Mira
- ☐ Mirage
- ☐ Neige
- ☐ Neve
- ☐ Nico
- ☐ Noe
- ☐ Pilar
- ☐ Rhea
- ☐ Roxy
- ☐ Saba
- ☐ Selena
- ☐ Selma
- ☐ Serena
- ☐ Shiloh
- ☐ Sejour
- ☐ Sidony
- ☐ Sudie
- ☐ Sukey
- ☐ Tempest
- ☐ Tezia
- ☐ Vada
- ☐ Vrai
- ☐ Woo
- ☐ Yasmine
- ☐ Xanthe
- ☐ Zade
- ☐ Zara
- ☐ Zelda
- ☐ Zen
- ☐ Zena
- ☐ Zenobia
- ☐ Zoozie
- ☐ Zola
- ☐ Zora

✳ The Cats

- ❏ Akeem
- ❏ Aldo
- ❏ Baz
- ❏ Benicio
- ❏ Boaz
- ❏ César
- ❏ Chaz
- ❏ Cicero
- ❏ Cruz
- ❏ Dax
- ❏ Django
- ❏ Elio
- ❏ Eno
- ❏ Enzo
- ❏ Ezra
- ❏ Gideon
- ❏ Gonzalo
- ❏ Guitar
- ❏ Helio
- ❏ Hombre
- ❏ Ishmael
- ❏ Jace
- ❏ Jamal
- ❏ Japhy

- ❏ Jasper
- ❏ Jesper
- ❏ Joaquin
- ❏ Kai
- ❏ Maceo
- ❏ Malik
- ❏ Marquis
- ❏ Orlando
- ❏ Rico
- ❏ Rio
- ❏ Rocco
- ❏ Roux
- ❏ Sayid
- ❏ Sergei
- ❏ Skate
- ❏ Taj
- ❏ Titus
- ❏ Xander
- ❏ Yoshi
- ❏ Zane
- ❏ Zeo
- ❏ Zeno
- ❏ Zion
- ❏ Zinc

Purr-sons of Interest

Cats possess many of the finer qualities of the human race: they're graceful, dramatic, thoughtful, athletic, and of course, extremely intelligent. If they didn't have to nap so often, there's no telling what they could achieve. Does your cat have a certain athletic leap that brings to mind the soaring bounds of a track and field star? A gesture that recalls Martha Graham in her prime? A certain wail that echoes Wagner's opera, RIDE OF THE VALKERIES? Consider a name from this collection of notable people, and your cat might just be inspired to follow in his namesake's footsteps.

Musicats

Caterwauling is an underappreciated musical form, as your cat is sure to let you know. Encourage your cat's natural attraction to music with a name from one of history's musicats.

- ❏ Abba
- ❏ Amadeus
- ❏ Bechet
- ❏ Bird
- ❏ Bix
- ❏ Berlioz
- ❏ Bowie
- ❏ Cab
- ❏ Callas
- ❏ Caruso
- ❏ Chopin
- ❏ Cher
- ❏ Coltrane
- ❏ Coolio
- ❏ Count Basie
- ❏ Dizzie
- ❏ Django
- ❏ DJ Spooky
- ❏ Dylan
- ❏ Ellington
- ❏ Elton
- ❏ Elvis

- ❏ Fats
- ❏ Fat Boy Slim
- ❏ Figaro
- ❏ Frescobaldi
- ❏ Handel
- ❏ Jagger
- ❏ Jellyroll
- ❏ J. Lo
- ❏ Jay-Z
- ❏ JoJo
- ❏ L.L Cool J.
- ❏ Liberace
- ❏ Liszt
- ❏ Madonna
- ❏ Mahalia
- ❏ Marley
- ❏ Marsalis
- ❏ Miles
- ❏ Mingus
- ❏ P. Diddy
- ❏ Prima
- ❏ Neville

- ❏ Prince
- ❏ Professor Longhair
- ❏ Paganini
- ❏ Puccini
- ❏ Rachmaninoff
- ❏ Rossini
- ❏ RuPaul
- ❏ Saffire
- ❏ Satchmo
- ❏ Scarlatti
- ❏ Slim Shady
- ❏ Strauss
- ❏ Schumann
- ❏ Sun Ra
- ❏ Thelonious
- ❏ Telemann
- ❏ Torme
- ❏ Veloso
- ❏ Verdi
- ❏ Wagner
- ❏ Yo Yo Ma
- ❏ Zappa

Musical Terms

☆ Aida
☆ Adagio
☆ Andante
☆ Aria
☆ Banjo
☆ Basso
☆ Blues
☆ Brio
☆ Calypso
☆ Cantata
☆ Caprice
☆ Crunk
☆ Groove
☆ Hip Hop
☆ Lyric
☆ Mamba
☆ Mambo
☆ Marimba
☆ Melody
☆ Oboe
☆ Piccolo
☆ Riff
☆ Sax
☆ Serenade
☆ Sonata
☆ Soprano
☆ Tango
☆ Tempo
☆ Trance
☆ Techno
☆ Tuba

Cat Stars

Bathe your cat in the glow of limelight with a name that calls to mind paparazzi, red carpets, and stretch limos. Hollywood, here she comes.

❏ Angelina
❏ Antonio
❏ Benicio
❏ Bing
❏ Cary Grant
❏ Gable
❏ Bardot
❏ Bergman
❏ Bertolucci
❏ Bogie
❏ Brando
❏ Chaplin

❏ Clint
❏ Clooney
❏ Cocteau
❏ Cooper
❏ Coppola
❏ Charlize
❏ DeCaprio
❏ Demi

- ❏ Denzel
- ❏ Ewan
- ❏ Garbo
- ❏ Goldie
- ❏ Gong Li
- ❏ Groucho
- ❏ Halle
- ❏ Hitchcock
- ❏ Harlow
- ❏ Harpo
- ❏ Hepburn
- ❏ Hopper
- ❏ James Dean
- ❏ Jackie Chan
- ❏ Jet Li
- ❏ Keanu
- ❏ Keira
- ❏ Kurosawa
- ❏ Kubrick
- ❏ Lamour
- ❏ Lucy Liu
- ❏ Marilyn
- ❏ Orlando
- ❏ Orson
- ❏ Pacino
- ❏ Scarlett
- ❏ Scorsese
- ❏ Sophia Loren
- ❏ Travolta
- ❏ Truffaut
- ❏ Uma
- ❏ Valentino

Shall We Dance?

- ☆ Ailey
- ☆ Balanchine
- ☆ Baryshnikov
- ☆ Fred
- ☆ Ginger
- ☆ Isadora
- ☆ Merce
- ☆ Nijinsky
- ☆ Nureyev
- ☆ Pavlova
- ☆ Twyla

Artisticats

Visually stunning, cats are themselves works of art. Modern or traditional, impressionistic or abstract, there's sure to be a name on this list that captures your cat's unique appearance and kinetic energy.

- ❑ Alto
- ❑ Ansel
- ❑ Arp
- ❑ Basquiat
- ❑ Botticelli
- ❑ Calder
- ❑ Caravaggio
- ❑ Cezanne
- ❑ Chihuily
- ❑ Dali

- ❑ Da Vinci
- ❑ Degas
- ❑ Delacroix
- ❑ Donatello
- ❑ Duchamp
- ❑ Eames
- ❑ Eero
- ❑ El Greco
- ❑ Frida
- ❑ Gaugin

- ❑ Gehry
- ❑ Haring
- ❑ Hiroshige
- ❑ Hockney
- ❑ Goya
- ❑ Kandinsky
- ❑ Klimt
- ❑ Longo
- ❑ Magritte
- ❑ Matisse
- ❑ Michelangelo
- ❑ Mies
- ❑ Miro
- ❑ Modigliani
- ❑ Modotti
- ❑ Monet
- ❑ Noguchi
- ❑ Raphael
- ❑ Rembrandt
- ❑ Renoir
- ❑ Rodin
- ❑ Picasso
- ❑ Sargent
- ❑ Steiglitz
- ❑ Titian
- ❑ Twombley
- ❑ Warhol
- ❑ Weegee
- ❑ Whistler
- ❑ Van Gogh
- ❑ Velázquez
- ❑ Vermeer

Prose and Poeticats

If only cats could type, what great works of literature they might create! As it is, we'll have to settle for the human perspective in literature. Fortunately, there's many an auteur worthy of lending his/her name to your pet. Is your cat the experimental type? Perhaps he's a Burroughs. Or more poetic? Byron might be a good choice. Peruse this list for a perfect NOM DE PURR.

- ❏ Albee
- ❏ Auden
- ❏ Austen
- ❏ Balzac
- ❏ Baudelaire
- ❏ Beckett
- ❏ Blake
- ❏ Boccaccio
- ❏ Burroughs
- ❏ Brontë
- ❏ Byron
- ❏ Camus
- ❏ Capote

- ❏ Casanova
- ❏ Cervantes
- ❏ Chekhov
- ❏ Chaucer
- ❏ Clancy
- ❏ Cocteau
- ❏ Colette
- ❏ Dante
- ❏ Dashiell
- ❏ Defoe
- ❏ Dickens
- ❏ Dostoyevsky
- ❏ Dumas

- ❏ Eliot
- ❏ Elmore
- ❏ Ezra
- ❏ Fitzgerald
- ❏ Flaubert
- ❏ Gide
- ❏ Goëthe
- ❏ Hardy
- ❏ Hemingway
- ❏ Hugo
- ❏ Ibsen
- ❏ Huxley
- ❏ Joyce

- ❏ Kafka
- ❏ Keats
- ❏ Kerouac
- ❏ Kesey
- ❏ Kipling
- ❏ Langston
- ❏ Longfellow
- ❏ Lorca
- ❏ Mamet
- ❏ Neruda
- ❏ Márquez
- ❏ Pepys
- ❏ Pinter

Athleticats

Recalling the leonine motions of their distant cousins, athleticats can run, pounce, and jump with grace and agility. Now if they could only catch fly balls, they'd really be in business. If your cat displays natural athletic ability, one of these major league names might be just the ticket.

❏ Poe
❏ Proust
❏ Rilke
❏ Rimbaud
❏ Rumi
❏ Salinger
❏ Saramago
❏ Sarte
❏ Seuss
❏ Shakespeare
❏ Shelley
❏ Tennessee
❏ Tennyson
❏ Thackeray
❏ Thoreau
❏ Tolkien
❏ Tolstoy
❏ Twain
❏ Whitman
❏ Wilde
❏ Woolf
❏ Wordsworth
❏ Yeats
❏ Zola

❏ Aggasi
❏ Ali
❏ Apolo
❏ Arantxa
❏ Babe Ruth
❏ Beckham
❏ Björn
❏ Jordan
❏ Kareem
❏ Katarina Witt
❏ Lance
❏ LeBron
❏ Magic
❏ Maradona

❏ Nomar
❏ Oksana
❏ Pelé
❏ Picabo
❏ Pippen
❏ Ripkin
❏ Ronaldinho
❏ Satchel
❏ Shaq
❏ Smokin' Joe
❏ Steffi
❏ Sugar Ray
❏ Tiger
❏ Venus

Scientificats

Where would science be with out the contributions of cats? Schrödinger's cat, for example, added much to the exploration of quantum mechanics. Schrödinger's friend Einstein used cats and their tails to help explain how the telegraph worked. Why not experiment with a scientific name for your cat?

- ❏ Archimedes
- ❏ Asimov
- ❏ Banneker
- ❏ Cassini
- ❏ Copernicus
- ❏ Cousteau
- ❏ Curie
- ❏ Darwin
- ❏ Doppler

- ❏ Edison
- ❏ Einstein
- ❏ Euclid
- ❏ Faraday
- ❏ Foucault
- ❏ Hubble
- ❏ Galileo
- ❏ Kepler

- ❏ Marconi
- ❏ Mendel
- ❏ Newton
- ❏ Ohm
- ❏ Pascal
- ❏ Pavlov
- ❏ Pliny
- ❏ Tesla
- ❏ Tycho

Think Cats

Cats have an uncanny ability to unravel the mysteries of the universe, or at least the mysteries of yarn balls (perhaps the two are more closely related than we think). While he's sitting in the window, soaking up the sun, your cat may well be constructing a new and important cosmic paradigm. A philosophical cat deservers an appropriate philosophical name, don't you think?

- ❏ Aristotle
- ❏ Cassius
- ❏ Cicero
- ❏ Confucius
- ❏ Descartes
- ❏ Freud
- ❏ Jung
- ❏ Kierkegaard
- ❏ Kant
- ❏ Machiavelli
- ❏ Nietzsche
- ❏ Ovid
- ❏ Philo

- ❏ Plato
- ❏ Plutarch
- ❏ Rousseau
- ❏ Sartre
- ❏ Seneca
- ❏ Siddhartha
- ❏ Socrates
- ❏ Spinoza
- ❏ Thoreau
- ❏ Virgil
- ❏ Voltaire

The Eternal Kitty

The ancient Egyptians knew it, and we know it, too: cats are simply divine, worthy of nothing less than worship. A god or goddess name is a perfect way to pay tribute to your cat's inner deity. That and supplying a daily offering of pats, scratches, and rubs.

FEMALE NAME	ORIGIN
❏ Anjea	Australian aboriginal fertility goddess
❏ Aphrodite	Greek goddess of love and beauty
❏ Artemis	Greek goddess of the hunt, wilderness
❏ Athena	Greek goddess of wisdom
❏ Aurora	Roman goddess of the dawn
❏ Bast or Bastet	Egyptian cat goddess
❏ Cait Sidhe	A feline creature in Celtic myth
❏ Camma	Celtic hunting goddess
❏ Cassandra	Greek prophetess
❏ Cassiopeia	Queen in Greek myth
❏ Ceres	Roman goddess of the harvest
❏ Chang'e	Chinese moon goddess
❏ Cybele	Greco-Roman mother goddess
❏ Damara	British fertility goddess
❏ Electra	Figure in Greek myth
❏ Danu	Anglo-Saxon mother goddess
❏ Eos	Greek goddess of the dawn
❏ Eris	Greek goddess of strife
❏ Freya	Norse fertility goddess
❏ Io	Figure in Greek myth
❏ Hathor	Egyptian Milky Way goddess
❏ Hera	Greek queen of the gods
❏ Inanna	Sumerian goddess
❏ Ishtar	Mesopotamian fertility goddess
❏ Isis	Egyptian goddess
❏ Juno	Roman queen of the gods
❏ Kali	Hindu goddess of death and destruction
❏ Kwan Yin Ma	Malaysian goddess of mercy
❏ Luna	Roman moon goddess
❏ Lalita	Hindu goddess of beauty
❏ Mama Cocha	Incan goddess of the sea
❏ Mama Zara	Incan fertility goddess
❏ Maya	Hindu goddess of illusion and mystery

FEMALE NAME	ORIGIN
❏ Minerva	Roman goddess of wisdom
❏ Morrigen	Celtic war goddess
❏ Mut	Egyptian mother goddess
❏ Nanna	Norse goddess
❏ Pandora	Figure in Greek myth
❏ Pasht	Alternative spelling of Bast, Egyptian goddess
❏ Pelé	Hawaiian volcano goddess
❏ Persephone	Greek goddess of the harvest
❏ Pinga	Inuit goddess of the hunt
❏ Rhiannon	Celtic moon goddess
❏ Pomona	Roman goddess of fruit trees
❏ Saraswati	Hindu goddess of wisdom
❏ Selene	Roman goddess of the moon
❏ Sekhmet	Egyptian goddess of lions
❏ Soma	Hindu moon deity
❏ Toci	Aztec earth goddess
❏ Ubasti	Alternative spelling of Bast, Egyptian goddess
❏ Venus	Roman goddess of love
❏ Vesta	Roman goddess of the hearth
❏ Wala	Australian aboriginal sun goddess
❏ Zeme	Slavic earth goddess

MALE NAME	ORIGIN
❑ Achilles	Greek hero
❑ Adonis	Greek god
❑ Ahti	Finnish god of lakes, streams
❑ Aeneus	Greek hero
❑ Amun	Egyptian creator deity
❑ Apollo	God of poetry, music, the sun
❑ Ajax	Greek hero
❑ Aries	Greek god of war
❑ Atlas	Figure in Greek myth
❑ Augustus	Roman emperor
❑ Balder	Norse god of beauty and light
❑ Bacchus	Roman god of wine
❑ Bast	Egyptian cat-bodied or cat-headed protector god
❑ Cai Shen	Chinese god of prosperity
❑ Cit Chac Coh	Mayan Puma god
❑ Cupid	Roman god of love
❑ Eduardo	Celtic god of perfection
❑ Geb	Egyptian earth god
❑ Ganesh	Hindu god of wisdom
❑ Helios	Greek god of the sun
❑ Hercules	Greek god of strength
❑ Hermes	Greek messenger of the gods
❑ Hypnos	Roman god of sleep
❑ Jade Emperor	Chinese ruler of the heavens
❑ Jupiter	Roman king of the gods
❑ Karora	Australian aboriginal creator god
❑ Khepry	Egyptian deity of the dawn, scarab beetle
❑ Lyr	Figure in Welsh mythology
❑ Loki	Trickster in Norse myth
❑ Midas	King from Greek myth

MALE NAME	ORIGIN
❏ Orpheus	Roman god of dreams
❏ Nanook	Inuit master of bears
❏ Neptune	Roman god of the sea
❏ Odin	Norse king of gods
❏ Orion	Figure from Greek myth
❏ Osiris	Egyptian god of the underworld
❏ Pan	God of forests
❏ Patripatan	Cat in Indian myth
❏ Peko	Estonian god of fertility
❏ Perseus	Greek hero
❏ Pikne	Estonian god of thunder
❏ Poseidon	Greek god of the seas
❏ Ra	Egyptian god known as "The Great Tomcat"
❏ Remus	Figure from Roman myth
❏ Romulus	Figure from Roman myth
❏ Septimus	Roman emperor
❏ Set	Egyptian god of storms
❏ Shiva	Hindu god of destruction
❏ Sobek	Egyptian crocodile god
❏ Thor	Norse god of thunder
❏ Ukko	Finnish god of thunder
❏ Vayu	Hindu god of wind
❏ Vulcan	Greek god of fire
❏ Zephyr	Greek god of wind
❏ Zao Jun	Chinese god of the kitchen
❏ Zeus	Greek king of gods

Cat Power

Cats have always made it clear that they don't really need humans around. They just indulge our presence. Many a cat has made a name for herself through intrepid acts and daring deeds. If you need a great name for your cat to live up to, consider one of these.

CAT	CLAIM TO FAME
❑ All Ball	The pet of Koko, the gorilla who could 'talk'
❑ Andy	Holds the cat record for non-fatal fall (200 feet [60 m])
❑ Blackberry	The first Munchkin cat
❑ Blackie	The richest cat in history (he inherited millions of British pounds)
❑ Brownie	Slightly less rich cat who inherited nearly half a million US dollars
❑ Bouhaki	Once believed to be the first cat with a name
❑ Copycat(CC)	The first cloned cat
❑ Faith	London cat who received a metal for bravery during WW II blitzkrieg
❑ Foss	Inspiration for *The Owl and the Pussycat*
❑ Fred	The Undercover Kitty, Famous for Assisting the NYPD and Brooklyn's District Attorney's Office
❑ Grampa	At 34, the oldest domestic cat ever recorded
❑ Hamlet	The world's most traveled cat, he flew approximately 372,822 miles (600,000 km) after getting stuck in a Canadian airplane for seven weeks.
❑ Hellcat	Cat who inherited close to half a million U.S. dollars
❑ Himmy	Held the record for heaviest cat at 46 lbs. (21km)
❑ Inga	Crew member at Mt. Washington Observatory

CAT	CLAIM TO FAME
❏ Kallibunker	One of the two founders of the Cornish Rex breed
❏ Kaspar	Wooden cat used at the Savoy Hotel in London to round out unlucky parties of 13
❏ Kinlee	Founding father of the Devon Rex breed
❏ Lewis	A Connecticut cat who was placed under house arrest
❏ Lipstick	Another pet cat "belonging" to Koko the gorilla
❏ Macavity	A British cat known for regularly catching a local bus by himself
❏ Mrs. Chippy	Member of the Ernest Shackleton expedition
❏ Morris II	Ran for U.S. president in 1988
❏ Mrs. Poodles	First Siamese cat shown at an English cat show, 1871
❏ Nedjem	Now regarded as the first cat known to have had a name
❏ Nin	Crew member at the Mt. Washington Observatory
❏ Pangur Bán	Inspired a poem by an early Irish monk

CAT	CLAIM TO FAME
❑ Peter	The Lord's (cricket club) cat, the only animal to have an obituary in Wisden Cricketers' Almanck
❑ Poppa	Second heaviest cat ever, weighed in at 44.5 lbs (20.2 kg)
❑ Scarlett	Saved her kittens from a fire in Brooklyn, New York
❑ Simon	Ship's cat of HMS Amethyst and the only cat to have won a medal for his rat-catching and morale-boosting activities
❑ Sinh	Founding father of the Birman breed
❑ Sugar	Followed his human family 1,500 miles (2,414 km)
❑ Tarawood Antigone	Holds the record for most kittens in one litter (19)
❑ Tibbles	Single-handedly wiped out the Stephens' Island Wren
❑ T.K.	Cat companion of Tondayelo, an orangutan
❑ Tinker Toy	Once held the record as smallest domestic cat known at 2.75 inches (7 cm) tall and 7.5 inches (19 cm) long
❑ Towser	Once held the record for most mice killed (over 28,000)
❑ The Unsinkable Sam	Mascot of the British Royal Navy who survived the torpedoing of three ships
❑ Wimauma	"Masterpiece of Chalsu" Cat's Magazine first "Cat of the Year"

The Cats of Purrsons of Note

Celebrities and people of note may seem to live in a different world, but at the end of the day they're just ordinary people, many of whom love cats just as much as you do. Take Ernest Hemingway—for example, he had 30 of them. And the French writer Colette: so devoted were her cats that it's said their decendents still replenish the flowers on her grave. A celebrity cat name might just bring a little panache into your world.

NAME	CELEBRITY
❏ Alice	Actor Martin Mull
❏ Ashley	TV host Vanna White
❏ Beelzebub	Mark Twain
❏ Beethoven	Martha Stewart
❏ Beppo	Lord Byron
❏ Bimbo	Artist Paul Klee
❏ Bing Clawsby	Radio host Michael Feinstein
❏ Bismarck	Florence Nightingale
❏ Blatherkite	Mark Twain
❏ Boche	Anne Frank

NAME	CELEBRITY
❏ Boise	Ernest Hemingway
❏ Boy	Vivien Leigh
❏ Buffalo Bill	Mark Twain
❏ Bunny Kitty	Actor Enrico Colantoni
❏ Cake	Warren Beatty
❏ Calvin	Writer Harriet Beecher Stowe
❏ Caruso	Singer Roberta Flack
❏ Catarina	Edgar Allan Poe
❏ Charo	Yoko Ono
❏ Cheeser	Jay Leno
❏ Chopin	F. Scott Fitzgerald
❏ Cobby	Author Thomas Hardy
❏ Dancer	Walter Cronkite
❏ Dillinger	Ernest Hemingway
❏ Delilah	Musician Freddie Mercury
❏ Disraeli	Florence Nightingale
❏ Dolly	Actress Tallulah Bankhead
❏ Dweezil	Actor Robert Wagner
❏ Ecstasy	Ernest Hemingway
❏ Elvis	John Lennon
❏ F. Puss	Ernest Hemingway
❏ Fatima	Playwright Horace Walpole
❏ Fats	Ernest Hemingway
❏ Fellini	Film critic Gene Shalit
❏ Fred	Cartoonist R. Crumb
❏ Friendless Brother	Ernest Hemingway
❏ Fritzi	Artist Paul Klee
❏ Furhouse	Ernest Hemingway
❏ Gavroche	Victor Hugo
❏ General Butchkin	Writer Iris Murdoch
❏ George Pushdragon	T.S. Eliot
❏ Giorgio	Philanthropist Peggy Guggenheim

NAME	CELEBRITY
❑ Gypsy	Peggy Guggenheim
❑ Hamilcar	Writer Anatole France
❑ Harold	Playwright Horace Walpole
❑ Hester	Andy Warhol
❑ Hodge	Essayist Dr. Samuel Johnson
❑ Jeepers Creepers	Elizabeth Taylor
❑ Jellylorum	T. S. Eliot
❑ Kapok	Writer Colette
❑ Kiki-la-Doucette	Colette
❑ La Chatte	Colette
❑ La Touteu	Colette
❑ Little Teddy	Enrico Colantoni
❑ Madame Vanity	Essayist Michel de Montaigne
❑ Magritte	Gloria Steinem
❑ Marcus	James Dean
❑ Marilyn Miste	Whitney Houston
❑ Master's Cat	Charles Dickens
❑ Meatball	Jane Pauley
❑ Mini-mini	Colette
❑ Minionne	Colette
❑ Minou	Writer George Sand

NAME	CELEBRITY
❏ Mirza Murad Alibeg	T.S. Eliot
❏ Misha	Yoko Ono
❏ Mitsou	Marilyn Monroe
❏ Moon	Actor Robert Wagner
❏ Mouche	Victor Hugo
❏ Mourka	Choreographer George Balanchine
❏ Mouschi	Anne Frank
❏ Mousetrap	Actor Van Heflin
❏ Murphy	Actress Bernadette Peters
❏ Muscat	Colette
❏ Mys	Paul Klee
❏ Mysouff	Writer Alexandre Dumas
❏ Nichols	Vivien Leigh
❏ Nightlife	Musician Charles Mingus
❏ Noilly Prat	T.S. Eliot
❏ Nuggi	Paul Klee
❏ Pascal	Anatole France
❏ Patapan	Horace Walpole
❏ Patsy	Charles Lindbergh
❏ Pattipaws	T.S. Eliot
❏ Poo Jones	Vivien Leigh
❏ Poppet	Joe Namath
❏ Pulcinella	Composer Domenico Scarlatti
❏ Punky	Doris Day
❏ Pyewacket	Actress Kim Novak
❏ Rhett Butler	TV host Vanna White
❏ Rita	Actress Julia Sweeney
❏ Romeo	Peggy Guggenheim
❏ Sam	Andy Warhol
❏ Samantha	Publisher Helen Gurley Brown
❏ Sara	Regis Philbin
❏ Sarah Snow	Writer Kingsley Amis
❏ Sasha	Yoko Ono

NAME	CELEBRITY
❏ Selima	Horace Walpole
❏ Sheba	Vivica A. Fox
❏ Silkhat	Van Heflin
❏ Simpkin	Poet Cecil Day-Lewis
❏ Sizi	Philosopher Albert Schweitzer
❏ Snookie	Vivica A. Fox
❏ Solomon	Writer Lloyd Alexander
❏ Sour Mash	Mark Twain
❏ Sweetface	Kim Gordon
❏ Taki	Raymond Chandler
❏ Tammany	Mark Twain
❏ Tantomile	T.S. Eliot
❏ Teeny	Martha Stewart
❏ Thruster	Ernest Hemingway
❏ Tiger	The Brontë Sisters
❏ Tiger	Aaron Neville
❏ Tigerlily	Actress Molly Ringwald
❏ Tigger	Vivica A. Fox
❏ Tommy	Anne Frank
❏ Topaz	Playwright Tennessee Williams
❏ Tuffy	Actress Ann-Margaret
❏ Turkey	Actress Janet Leigh
❏ Verdi	Martha Stewart
❏ Vivaldi	Martha Stewart
❏ Weasel	Cyndi Lauper
❏ Wilhelmina	Charles Dickens
❏ Willie	Comedian George Burns
❏ Wiscus	T.S. Eliot
❏ Zara	Horace Walpole
❏ Zoë	Painter Gabriele Rossetti
❏ Zoroaster	Mark Twain
❏ Zwerg	Colette

Politicats

Cats have always moved stealthily through the halls of power. Special advisers to those at the very top, they've had the ear and the lap of some of history's most infulencial

people. If your cat is a political animal, one of these names might get the vote.

NAME	POLITICAL FIGURE
❑ Ahmedabad	U.S. statesman John Kenneth Galbraith
❑ Blackie	Winston Churchill, and U.S President Calvin Coolidge
❑ Cleo	U.S. President Ronald Reagan
❑ Gris-Gris	Charles de Gaulle
❑ Humphrey	Cat who lived at the British prime minister's residence at 10 Downing Street during John Major's tenure
❑ India "Willie" Bush	U.S. President George W. Bush
❑ Jock	Winston Churchill
❑ Lady Arabella	John Spencer Churchill (Winston's son)
❑ Luck	King Charles I

❑ Margate	Winston Churchill
❑ Micette	Pope Leo XII
❑ Mimi-Paillon	Cardinal Richelieu
❑ Misty Malarky Ying Yang	U.S. President Jimmy Carter
❑ Myobu No Omoto	Emperor Ichijo of Japan
❑ Nelson	Winston Churchill
❑ Nemo	British Prime Minister Harold Wilson
❑ Princess Sophie Louise	John Spencer Churchill
❑ Prudence	Prime Minister Georges Clemenceau of France
❑ Sara	U.S. President Ronald Reagan
❑ Serpolet	Cardinal Richelieu
❑ Shuang-mei	Emperor Chu Hou-Tsung
❑ Siam	U.S. President Rutherford B. Hayes
❑ Slippers	U.S. President Theodore Roosevelt
❑ Socks	U.S. President Bill Clinton
❑ Tabby	U.S. President Abraham Lincoln's son Tad's cat (the first White House cat)
❑ Thisbe	Cardinal Richelieu
❑ Tom Quartz	U.S. President Theodore Roosevelt
❑ Tiger	U.S. President Calvin Coolidge
❑ Timmy	U.S. President Calvin Coolidge
❑ Vashka	Czar Nicholas I
❑ White Heather	Queen Victoria

Cosmic Kitty

As cat lovers are well aware, cats exist on a higher plane of consciousness than humans. Shape shifting, witchcraft, and magic—they're all part of the feline mystique. If your cat has that certain squint in her eyes that says, "Excuse me for a moment. I'm receiving a psychic transmission," you might just consider one of the names on this list. They're simply enchanting.

- Alberic
- Alchemy
- Amulet
- Aquarius
- Artemis
- Astra
- Aura
- Bellatrix
- Calypso
- Capricorn
- Cassiopeia
- Celeste
- Circe
- Crystal
- Diana
- Deva
- Djinn
- East
- Elphaba
- Elvira
- Enchantress
- Endora
- Esmeralda
- Exciter
- Fortuna
- Gaia
- Gemini
- Glinda
- Grimalkin
- Hephzibah
- Hecate
- Hex
- Idduna
- Isis
- Jadis
- Jinx
- Kali
- Libra
- Loiosh
- Luna
- Magic
- Magrat
- Maleficus
- Malkin
- Mawkin
- Meb
- Merlin
- Minerva
- Moonbeam
- Moonfire
- Moonstone
- Morgana
- Mystic
- Mysticat
- Mystique
- Narcissa
- Nymphia
- Oberon
- Ouija
- Pisces
- Pigwidgeon
- Quicksilver
- Sab
- Sabrina
- Sabotabby
- Samantha
- Samhain
- Scobax
- Scorpio
- Seraphina
- Shadowcat
- Shaman
- Sorceress
- Solstice
- Spirit
- Starbright
- Stardust
- Stargazer
- Strega
- Strix
- Talisman
- Tabitha
- Tarot
- Tatiana
- Taurus
- Teekl
- Tempest
- Wicca
- Zoraida

Cat. Food

Cats are natural gourmets. They may be forced by necessity to eat store-bought cat food, but most would prefer sashimi-grade tuna and caviar. Consider one of these gastronomically correct names for your feline foodie, each with its own distinctive flavor.

Tasty Treats

- ❑ Ambrosia
- ❑ Bisque
- ❑ Bonbon
- ❑ Bleubry
- ❑ Bocconcino
- ❑ Brie
- ❑ Capers
- ❑ Caramel
- ❑ Caviar
- ❑ Cayenne
- ❑ Cazuela
- ❑ Chai
- ❑ Chili
- ❑ Chapati
- ❑ Chicory
- ❑ Cider
- ❑ Cioppino
- ❑ Cinnamon
- ❑ Cocoa
- ❑ Coffee
- ❑ Cola
- ❑ Comté
- ❑ Coulis
- ❑ Curry
- ❑ Dijon
- ❑ Dobosch
- ❑ Edam
- ❑ Étouffée
- ❑ Evora
- ❑ Fondue
- ❑ Garbanzo

- ❑ Ginger
- ❑ Ginseng
- ❑ Gouda
- ❑ Guava
- ❑ Gumbo
- ❑ Hamachi
- ❑ Java
- ❑ Kiwi
- ❑ Kona
- ❑ Kumquat
- ❑ Latte
- ❑ Licorice
- ❑ Maguro
- ❑ Marmalade
- ❑ Marjoram
- ❑ Mascarpone
- ❑ Marzipan
- ❑ Masala
- ❑ Marshmallow
- ❑ Mignon
- ❑ Mimolette
- ❑ Miso
- ❑ Mocha
- ❑ Mutsu
- ❑ Muffin
- ❑ Muffelata
- ❑ Nilla
- ❑ Nougat
- ❑ Nutmeg
- ❑ Olive
- ❑ Panettone

- ❑ Paprika
- ❑ Pâte
- ❑ Pavlova
- ❑ Persimmon
- ❑ Pho
- ❑ Queso
- ❑ Quiche
- ❑ Radicchio
- ❑ Roquefort
- ❑ Saffron
- ❑ Salsa
- ❑ Samosa
- ❑ Sashimi
- ❑ Sassafras
- ❑ Sesame
- ❑ Sherbet
- ❑ Sorbet
- ❑ Splenda
- ❑ Sushi
- ❑ Tartine
- ❑ Taro
- ❑ Tikka
- ❑ Tilsit
- ❑ Tiramisu
- ❑ Truffle
- ❑ Tofu
- ❑ Vindaloo
- ❑ Wasabi
- ❑ Winesap

Spirits

- Absinthe
- Amaretto
- Beaujolais
- Boudreaux
- Bouschet
- Calvados
- Cassis
- Chianti
- Cognac
- Cointreau
- Corvina
- Courvoisier
- Daiquiri
- Dolcetto
- Frangelico
- Galliano
- Gimlet
- Grenache
- Julep
- Kahlúa
- Kir

- Limoncello
- Pernod
- Pinot
- Madiera
- Macabeo
- Madras
- Malbec
- Mauzac
- Mai tai
- Martini
- Merlot
- Midori
- Mimosa
- Mojito
- Mondeuce
- Moonshine
- Muscadelle
- Muscat
- Orangina
- Ouzo
- Palomino

- Pastis
- Pinotage
- Sambuca
- Sake
- Sangria
- Semillon
- Sherry
- Shiraz
- Smirnoff
- Spumante
- Soju
- Sousão
- Sultana
- Tarrango
- Tequila
- Toddy
- Tokay
- Trebbiano
- Verdicchio
- Xarello

Love Cats

Who says cats aren't affectionate? Anybody who's felt that furry swish around the ankles or heard the lovely purr of a contented cat knows that beneath that seemingly unruffled fur beats the heart of a true romantic. Don't hold back on showing your kitty you care—choose one of these unabashedly adoring nicknames and watch how she bathes you in sandpaper-tongue kisses.

- ❏ Amoré
  (Italian for love)
- ❏ Amor
- ❏ Angel
- ❏ Baby
- ❏ Baci
  (Italian for kisses)
- ❏ Bebé
- ❏ Babs
- ❏ Babykins
- ❏ Bambino
- ❏ Bitsy
- ❏ Bitty
- ❏ Blinky
- ❏ Bobo
- ❏ Boo
- ❏ Boo Boo
- ❏ Bootsie
- ❏ Buffy
- ❏ Catkin
- ❏ Chiquita (o)
  (Spanish for
  little one)

- ❏ Ciccia (o)
  (Italian for sweetie)
- ❏ Conlechita (o)
  (Spanish for coffee
  with milk)
- ❏ Corazon
  (Spanish for heart)
- ❏ Cosy
- ❏ Cuddles
- ❏ Cupcake
- ❏ Curly
- ❏ Cutie Pie
- ❏ Deary
- ❏ Dinky
- ❏ Dolly
- ❏ Ducky
- ❏ Gattina (o)
  (Spanish for kitty)
- ❏ Honey

- Itty
- Kiki
- KitKat
- Liebshen
  (German for baby)
- Little Bit
- Lolly
- Lovey
- Mamzelle
- Mew Mew
- Mewsy
- Mimi
- Mimsy
- Missy
- Moppet
- Mopsy
- Peaches
- Peanut
- Petit chou
  (French for little cabbage)
- Pinky
- Pip
- Pippa
- Pippi
- Pitty
- Pitty Pat
- Pompom
- Pookie
- Poquita (o)
- Precious
- Puddy
- Puffy
- Purrdy
- Puss Puss
- Snookie
- Silky
- Sir Purrsalot
- Sissy
- Skitty
- Smootch
- Snugglepuss
- Squeaky
- Squeegee
- Sugar
- Sweetpea
- Sweetie
- Taffy
- Teeny
- Tickles
- Tiny
- Twinkles
- Winky
- Winkles

Note: Names ending in o
are the masculine form.

Wild Cats

No matter how domesticated cats may be, there's still a hint of something wild in them. Honor your cat's inner feral feline with a name from nature. Earth, air, fire, and water—names from all the elements are included here. Choose a name that will make your kitty feel like a mighty jungle cat, even if he's just prowling the garden.

- ❏ Acacia
- ❏ Acanthus
- ❏ Amaranth
- ❏ Amaryllis
- ❏ Ambra
- ❏ Anise
- ❏ Apple
- ❏ Arjuna
- ❏ Arnica
- ❏ August
- ❏ Aurora
- ❏ Azalea
- ❏ Baobab
- ❏ Balsam
- ❏ Barley
- ❏ Begonia
- ❏ Belladonna
- ❏ Blackberry
- ❏ Blizzard
- ❏ Blossom
- ❏ Blueberry
- ❏ Breeze
- ❏ Briar
- ❏ Buttercup
- ❏ Calyx

- ❏ Chamomile
- ❏ Clary
- ❏ Clove
- ❏ Clover
- ❏ Cypress
- ❏ Celsia
- ❏ Calendula
- ❏ Comet
- ❏ Daffodil
- ❏ Dahlia
- ❏ Daisy
- ❏ Damiana
- ❏ Diamond
- ❏ Dove
- ❏ Ebony
- ❏ Eclipse
- ❏ Echo
- ❏ Emerald
- ❏ Étoile
  (French for star)
- ❏ Elysium
- ❏ Estrella
  (Spanish for star)
- ❏ Feather
- ❏ Fern

- ❏ Fire
- ❏ Flame
- ❏ Fleur
  (French for flower)
- ❏ Flint
- ❏ Forsythia
- ❏ Freesia
- ❏ Fuchsia
- ❏ Gardenia
- ❏ Garnet
- ❏ Hazel
- ❏ Henna
- ❏ Holly
- ❏ Hyacinth
- ❏ Iantha
- ❏ Ibis
- ❏ Ice
- ❏ Indigo
- ❏ Iris
- ❏ Ivy
- ❏ Immortelle
- ❏ Juniper
- ❏ Kamala
- ❏ Kiwi
- ❏ Lantana

- ❏ Lapis
- ❏ Lavender
- ❏ Lightning
- ❏ Lilac
- ❏ Lobelia
- ❏ Lotus
- ❏ Luna
- ❏ Magnolia
- ❏ Marigold
- ❏ Mariposa
  (Spanish
  for butterfly)
- ❏ Meadow
- ❏ Mica
- ❏ Midnight

- ❏ Mimosa
- ❏ Misty
- ❏ Moonlight
- ❏ Moonglow
- ❏ Myrtle
- ❏ Myrrh
- ❏ Narcissus
- ❏ Ocean
- ❏ Oleander
- ❏ Olive
- ❏ Onyx
- ❏ Opal
- ❏ Orchid
- ❏ Ophrys

- ❏ Pansy
- ❏ Patchouli
- ❏ Peony
- ❏ Periwinkle
- ❏ Petal
- ❏ Petunia
- ❏ Plum
- ❏ Plumeria
- ❏ Poppy
- ❏ Posey
- ❏ Printemps
  (French
  for spring)
- ❏ Rain
- ❏ Rainbow

- Raspberry
- Rosebud
- Ruby
- Raven
- River
- Sage
- Sassafras
- Shadow
- Shade
- Sky
- Snowflake
- Soleil
  (French for sun)
- Summer
- Sunny
- Sunshine
- Stormy
- Star
- Tansy
- Tangerine
- Thunder
- Twilight
- Twister
- Topaz
- Violet
- Willow
- Windy
- Zinnia

Famous Wild Cats

☆	Ba-tou	Writer Colette's African Wildcat
☆	Chiquita	Entertainer Josephine Baker's pet cheetah
☆	Elsa	Lioness from the *Born Free* books
☆	Italia	Benito Mussolini's pet lioness
☆	Penny	Leopard from *The Spotted Sphinx*
☆	Pippa	Cheetah from *Pippa the Cheetah and her Cubs*
☆	Smokey	U.S. President Calvin Coolidge's pet bobcat

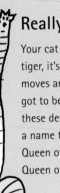

Really Wild Cats

Your cat is so in touch with her inner tiger, it's spooky. With her stealthy moves and lightning-fast pounce, she's got to be more than half panther. If these descriptions fit your cat, consider a name that reflects her position as Queen of the Jungle, even if she's only Queen of the Living Room.

☆ Bobcat
☆ Catopuma
☆ Caracal
☆ Cheetah
☆ Colocolo
☆ Cougar
☆ Jaguarundi
☆ Jaguar
☆ Jungle Cat
☆ Kodkod
☆ Liger
☆ Lion
☆ Leopard
☆ Lynx

☆ Margay
☆ Mountain lion
☆ Ocelot
☆ Oncilla
☆ Onza
☆ Pallas's cat
☆ Pampas cat
☆ Panther
☆ Puma
☆ Serval
☆ Tiger
☆ Wildcat

Gritty Kitties

The glamorous and sophisticated house cat is just one side of the story. In the mean streets of the world, the fierce, rangy alley cat lurks, ready to start a catfight with anybody who looks at him wrong. If your precious pet is in touch with his inner street fighter, consider a name from this list. Or choose one for your delicate creature—it might just be the touch of irony you're looking for.

- ☐ Ace
- ☐ Alley Cat
- ☐ Alpha
- ☐ Attila
- ☐ Attack
- ☐ Blade
- ☐ Blitz
- ☐ Brave
- ☐ Bravo
- ☐ Chief
- ☐ Catastrophe
- ☐ Claws
- ☐ Cruella
- ☐ Destructo
- ☐ Fang
- ☐ Fat Cat
- ☐ Flea
- ☐ Fleabag
- ☐ Hanibal
- ☐ Harpy
- ☐ Hellcat
- ☐ Hissy
- ☐ Howl
- ☐ Hunter
- ☐ Icky
- ☐ Kamikaze
- ☐ Litter
- ☐ Lucifer
- ☐ Magnum
- ☐ Maleficence
- ☐ Medusa
- ☐ Mephisto
- ☐ Mess
- ☐ Ninja
- ☐ Panzer
- ☐ Ranger
- ☐ Rambo
- ☐ Rocky
- ☐ Rocco
- ☐ Rocket
- ☐ Scram
- ☐ Screech
- ☐ Scrounger
- ☐ Sher Khan
- ☐ Smelly Cat
- ☐ Psycho
- ☐ Sarge
- ☐ Samurai
- ☐ Scab
- ☐ Scar
- ☐ Scaredy
- ☐ Scat
- ☐ Scratch
- ☐ Sour Puss
- ☐ Spike
- ☐ Stray
- ☐ Trouble
- ☐ Yowl

Notorious C.A.T.s

☆	The Champawat Tigress	Tigress that killed over 400 people
☆	The Darkness	Tsavo maneater that killed over 100 Kenyans
☆	The Ghost	Tsavo maneater that killed over 100 Kenyans
☆	The Panar Leopard	Leopard that killed 400 people
☆	The Thak Tigress	Famous man-eating tigress

A Great Purr-sonality

Choosing the right name for your cat might be easier than you think. If you study him closely the way he studies you—the distinctive way he moves, purrs, and plays—the purrfect name might just pounce on you.

- ❏ Archie
- ❏ Bonkers
- ❏ Bouncy
- ❏ Bubbles
- ❏ Charmant
- ❏ Chatty
- ❏ Chat Cat
- ❏ Cheeky
- ❏ Cheery
- ❏ Cozy
- ❏ Crazy
- ❏ Crook
- ❏ Curious
- ❏ Dancer
- ❏ Dash
- ❏ Dasher
- ❏ Devil
- ❏ Diablito
- ❏ Dreamy
- ❏ Emo
- ❏ Firecracker
- ❏ Felina
- ❏ Finicky
- ❏ Flash
- ❏ Freaky
- ❏ Flirt
- ❏ Flirty
- ❏ Fraidy
- ❏ Fussy
- ❏ Gabby
- ❏ Gracey
- ❏ Goofy
- ❏ Hackles
- ❏ Happy Cat
- ❏ Hissy
- ❏ Hoover
- ❏ Hunter
- ❏ Kneady
- ❏ Leo
- ❏ Leona
- ❏ Loca (o)
- ❏ Lucky
- ❏ Macho
- ❏ Magnum
- ❏ Master
- ❏ Minx
- ❏ Moocher
- ❏ Moody
- ❏ Miu Miu
- ❏ Mr./Miss /Mrs./ Ms. Crankypaws
- ❏ Mr./Miss/ Mrs/ Ms. Grumpus
- ❏ Party Cat
- ❏ Perky
- ❏ Phantom
- ❏ Picky
- ❏ Piddy Pat
- ❏ Playful
- ❏ Pouncer
- ❏ Prowly
- ❏ Prowler
- ❏ Puddles
- ❏ Pussyfoot
- ❏ Queenie
- ❏ Randy
- ❏ Rangy
- ❏ Romeo
- ❏ Rowdy
- ❏ Sassy
- ❏ Scooter
- ❏ Shy Shy
- ❏ Show Off
- ❏ Skittles
- ❏ Slinky
- ❏ Snarf
- ❏ Sneakers
- ❏ Sneaky
- ❏ Sparky

- ❏ Star
- ❏ Stealthy
- ❏ Sugar
- ❏ Sweetie
- ❏ Swishy
- ❏ Sweet Pea
- ❏ Tailchaser
- ❏ Tricky
- ❏ Trixie
- ❏ Trouble
- ❏ Trusty
- ❏ Tuffy
- ❏ Tussy
- ❏ Twitchy
- ❏ Twitchaba
- ❏ Twinkles
- ❏ Wanderer
- ❏ Watchcat
- ❏ Whiny
- ❏ Whisper
- ❏ Zen
- ❏ Zoomer
- ❏ Zoomy

Note: Names ending in o are the masculine form.

Don't Call Them Lazy—
They're Just Relaxed

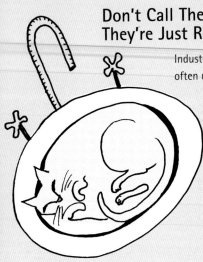

Industrious is not among the adjectives often used to describe cats. That's just fine by them—they've got nine lives, and they intend to enjoy every one of them. If your cat has that certain languorous demeanor, mull over one of these monikers.

☆ Bum
☆ Bumsy
☆ Couch Potato
☆ Dorma
☆ Dormant
☆ Dozy
☆ Drowsy
☆ Dude
☆ Gavroche
☆ Hypnos
☆ Idelle
☆ Lackadaisy
☆ Mr./Miss/Mrs./Ms. Lazy Bones
☆ Lazy Daisy
☆ Lazy Susan
☆ Loaf
☆ Lolly
☆ Lollygagger
☆ Lounge Cat
☆ Lumpy
☆ Morpheus

☆ Napper
☆ Nappy
☆ Nebbish
☆ Nelly
☆ Nod
☆ Paresseux (French for lazy)
☆ Perezoso (Spanish for lazy)
☆ Pigro (Italian for lazy)
☆ Pokey
☆ Schläfrig (German for sleepy)
☆ Siesta
☆ Slacker
☆ Släperig (Dutch for sleepy)
☆ Sleepy
☆ Sloth
☆ Slouch
☆ Slug
☆ Slo Mo
☆ Snoozer
☆ Snoozy
☆ Soma

Splendi-fur-ous

A cat's coat is her crowning glory. The color, texture, and sheen of her fur are the first things people notice about her and are a big part of what makes her unique. Why not honor your cat's fabulous fur with a name that calls it like it is? Looks may not be everything, but they're a great place to start when looking for a cat name.

- Baldy
- Bella
- Blacky
- Bluey
- Brindle
- Boucle
- Brilliantine
- Carbon
- Cashmere
- Chamois
- Charmeuse
- Chenille
- Chessie
- Chiffon
- Chestnut
- Chinchilla
- Chocolate
- Cinder
- Cobby
- Dimity
- Dandy
- Dotty
- Duffer
- Dusty
- Ebony
- Ermine
- Fancy
- Fatty
- Feather
- Fleck
- Freckles
- Fleecey
- Floofy
- Fluff

- Fluffy
- Frisky
- Frou Frou
- Furry
- Furball
- Fuzzy
- Ghosty
- Gris Gris
- Honey
- Inky
- Ivory
- Jet
- Kohl
- Lacy
- Lamby
- Lamé
- Lux
- Mackerel
- Marshmallow
- Merino
- Midnight
- Mittens
- Mocha
- Moggy
- Mohair
- Money
- Nappy
- Neige
- Onyx
- Oreo
- Pashmina
- Patchy
- Pepper
- Piebald

- Puff
- Puffy
- Putty
- Ruby
- Rusty
- Sable
- Satin
- Scruffy
- Sable
- Shadow
- Shaggy
- Shantung
- Sienna
- Silky
- Skinny
- Sleeky
- Smoky
- Smoothy
- Smudge
- Sneakers
- Snowy
- Softy
- Stripey
- Tabby
- Tawny
- Tickle
- Torbie
- Tortie
- Umber
- Velvet
- Velveteen
- Whitey

Sophisticats

If there were a class system in the animal kingdom, cats would surely be at the top of it. With their superior intelligence, good taste, and refined manners, they possess all the qualities that most animals can only aspire to. Consider a name that says "impeccable breeding." These top-drawer monikers simply ooze sophistication—what could be more fitting for your noble little beast?

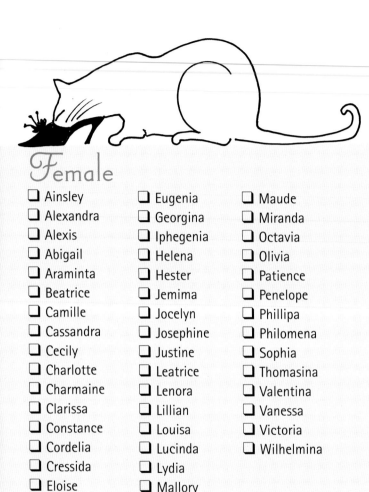

Female

- [ ] Ainsley
- [ ] Alexandra
- [ ] Alexis
- [ ] Abigail
- [ ] Araminta
- [ ] Beatrice
- [ ] Camille
- [ ] Cassandra
- [ ] Cecily
- [ ] Charlotte
- [ ] Charmaine
- [ ] Clarissa
- [ ] Constance
- [ ] Cordelia
- [ ] Cressida
- [ ] Eloise
- [ ] Elspeth

- [ ] Eugenia
- [ ] Georgina
- [ ] Iphegenia
- [ ] Helena
- [ ] Hester
- [ ] Jemima
- [ ] Jocelyn
- [ ] Josephine
- [ ] Justine
- [ ] Leatrice
- [ ] Lenora
- [ ] Lillian
- [ ] Louisa
- [ ] Lucinda
- [ ] Lydia
- [ ] Mallory
- [ ] Mathilde

- [ ] Maude
- [ ] Miranda
- [ ] Octavia
- [ ] Olivia
- [ ] Patience
- [ ] Penelope
- [ ] Phillipa
- [ ] Philomena
- [ ] Sophia
- [ ] Thomasina
- [ ] Valentina
- [ ] Vanessa
- [ ] Victoria
- [ ] Wilhelmina

Male

- Alexander
- Ambrose
- Archibald
- Augustus
- Basil
- Bertram
- Carleton
- Cecil
- Cedric
- Chadwick
- Chandler
- Chanticleer
- Chauncey
- Colby
- Constantine
- Cornelius
- Dirk

- Dudley
- Edmund
- Forrest
- Gavin
- Giles
- Godfrey
- Gustaf
- Heathcliff
- Hunter
- Jeeves
- Julian
- Julius
- Lucien
- Magnus
- Malcolm
- Nash
- Nigel
- Octavius

- Oscar
- Otto
- Pier
- Raphael
- Reginald
- Rhys
- Rollo
- Rupert
- Savion
- Sebastian
- Sheldon
- Sinjin
- Simeon
- Tristan
- Victor
- Winton
- Winston
- Zachary

Duplicats and Triplicats

Cats are so fabulous, it's not surprising that many people live with more than one. Two is common, three not terribly unusual, four...well, that's when eyebrows raise (as if you cared!). These names are great for dynamic duos or terrific threesomes. For a quartet, you're on your own.

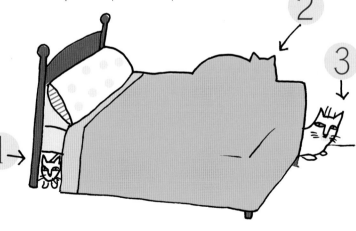

Males and Females

- ❏ Abercrombie and Fitch
- ❏ Alsace and Lorraine
- ❏ Apples and Oranges
- ❏ Asterisk and Obelisk
- ❏ Bacon and Eggs
- ❏ Bada Bing and Bada Boom
- ❏ Bangers and Mash
- ❏ Barnes and Noble
- ❏ Beauty and Beast
- ❏ Biscuits and Gravy
- ❏ Black and White
- ❏ Bright Eyes and Bushy Tail
- ❏ Bread and Butter
- ❏ Bubble and Squeak
- ❏ Calvin and Hobbes
- ❏ Cake and Ice Cream
- ❏ Cheese and Crackers
- ❏ Chip and Dale
- ❏ Chicken and Biscuit
- ❏ Chicken and Dumplings
- ❏ Chips and Dip
- ❏ Chips and Salsa
- ❏ Click and Clack
- ❏ Cloak and Dagger
- ❏ Crimson and Clover
- ❏ Cut and Paste
- ❏ Diamonds and Pearls
- ❏ Ebony and Ivory
- ❏ Fish and Chips
- ❏ Flotsam and Jetsam
- ❏ Frank and Beans
- ❏ Gumby and Pokey
- ❏ Harley and Davidson
- ❏ Heaven and Earth
- ❏ Itchy and Scratchy
- ❏ Jeepers and Creepers
- ❏ Kit and Caboodle
- ❏ Lettuce and Tomato
- ❏ Lilo and Stitch
- ❏ Minneapolis and St. Paul
- ❏ Milk and Cookies
- ❏ Mutt and Jeff

- ❏ Night and Day
- ❏ Oil and Vinegar
- ❏ Oil and Water
- ❏ Peaches and Cream
- ❏ Peanut Butter and Jelly
- ❏ Pinky and the Brain
- ❏ Pitter and Patter
- ❏ Pork and Beans
- ❏ Ren and Stimpy
- ❏ Rocky and Bullwinkle
- ❏ St. Kitts and Nevis
- ❏ Salt and Pepper

- ❏ Spaghetti and Meatballs
- ❏ Sugar and Spice
- ❏ Tea and Cakes
- ❏ Tea and Toast
- ❏ Timon and Pumbaa
- ❏ Trinidad and Tobago
- ❏ Turks and Caicos
- ❏ Tweedledee and Tweedledum
- ❏ Vanilla and Chocolate
- ❏ Wine and Cheese
- ❏ Yin and Yang

He Cats

- ❏ Abbott and Costello
- ❏ Amos and Andy
- ❏ Batman and Robin
- ❏ Ben and Jerry
- ❏ Bert and Ernie
- ❏ Bill and Ted
- ❏ Cheech and Chong
- ❏ Currier and Ives
- ❏ Felix and Oscar
- ❏ Fred and Barney
- ❏ Frick and Frack
- ❏ Frodo and Sam
- ❏ Gilbert and Sullivan
- ❏ Harold and Kumar
- ❏ Holmes and Watson
- ❏ Jake and Elwood
- ❏ Jay and Silent Bob
- ❏ Jeeves and Wooster
- ❏ Jekyll and Hyde
- ❏ Kirk and Spock
- ❏ Leopold and Loeb
- ❏ Laurel and Hardy
- ❏ Lenny and Squiggy
- ❏ Lennon and McCartney
- ❏ Lewis and Clark
- ❏ Mason and Dickson Dixon
- ❏ Penn and Teller
- ❏ Rodgers and Hammerstein
- ❏ Rogers and Hart
- ❏ Sam and Dave
- ❏ Shrek and Donkey
- ❏ Siegfried and Roy
- ❏ Simon and Garfunkel
- ❏ Siskel and Ebert
- ❏ Sly and Robbie
- ❏ Starsky and Hutch
- ❏ Tom and Jerry
- ❏ Wallace and Gromit
- ❏ Wilbur and Orville
- ❏ Woodward and Bernstein

She Cats

- ❏ Aly and AJ
- ❏ Betty and Veronica
- ❏ Cagney and Lacey
- ❏ Electrowoman and Dynagirl
- ❏ Gertrude and Alice B
- ❏ Ginger and Mary Ann
- ❏ Helena and Hermia
  (*Midsummer Night's Dream*)
- ❏ Kate and Alley

- ❑ Laverne and Shirley
- ❑ Lucy and Ethel
- ❑ Mary-Kate and Ashley
- ❑ Paris and Nicole
- ❑ Patsy and Edina
- ❑ Salt and Pepa
- ❑ Thelma and Louise
- ❑ Tea and Crumpets
- ❑ Tia and Tamera
- ❑ Trinny and Susannah
- ❑ Venus and Serena
- ❑ Whistles and Bells
- ❑ Wilma and Betty
- ❑ Wynona and Naomi
- ❑ Xena and Gabrielle
- ❑ Zsa Zsa and Eva

ℋe Cats and She Cats

- ❑ Adam and Eve
- ❑ Aladdin and Jasmine
- ❑ Anthony and Cleopatra
- ❑ Barbie and Ken
- ❑ Bogie and Bacall
- ❑ Bonnie and Clyde
- ❑ Boris and Natasha
- ❑ Burns and Allen
- ❑ Dick and Jane
- ❑ Fred and Ginger
- ❑ Hagar and Helga
- ❑ Hansel and Gretel
- ❑ Harold and Maude
- ❑ He-Man and She-Ra
- ❑ Homer and Marge
- ❑ Lady and Tramp
- ❑ Lucy and Desi
- ❑ Mickey and Minnie
- ❑ Nicholas and Alexandra
- ❑ Othello and Desdemona
- ❑ Ozzie and Harriet
- ❑ Popeye and Olive Oyl
- ❑ Porgy and Bess
- ❑ Posh and Becks
- ❑ Raggedy Ann
    and Raggedy Andy
- ❑ Regis and Kathy Lee
- ❑ Rhett and Scarlett
- ❑ Romeo and Juliet
- ❑ Samson and Delilah
- ❑ Scully and Mulder
- ❑ Sid and Nancy
- ❑ Shrek and Fiona
- ❑ Sonny and Cher
- ❑ Tarzan and Jane
- ❑ Tracy and Hepburn
- ❑ Will and Grace

Triplicats

- Aglaia, Euphrosyne, and Thalia (The Three Graces)
- Alvin, Simon, and Theodore (The Chipmunks)
- Athos, Porthos, and Aramis (The Three Musketeers)
- Atropos, Clotho, and Lachesis (The Fates)
- Bacon, Lettuce, and Tomato
- Betsy, Tacy, and Tib
- Caesar, Anthony, and Cleopatra
- Charlotte, Emily, and Ann (Bronte)
- Earth, Wind, and Fire
- Good, Bad, Ungly
- Gold, Frankincense, and Myrrh
- Gold, Silver, and Bronze
- Hickory, Dickory, and Dock
- Hop, Skip, and Jump
- Faith, Hope, and Charity
- Flora, Fauna, and Meriwether
- Flopsy, Mopsy, and Cottontail
- Harry, Ron, and Hermione
- Hook, Line, and Sinker
- Huey, Louey, and Dewey
- Larry, Moe, and Curly
- Lights, Camera, and Action
- Morning, Noon, and Night
- Peter, Paul, and Mary
- Ready, Willing, and Able
- Red, White, and Blue
- Rock, Paper, and Scissors
- Sex, Drugs, and Rock 'n Roll
- Shake, Rattle, and Roll
- Snap, Crackle, and Pop
- Tic, Tac, and Toe
- Tom, Dick, and Harry
- Wynken, Blyken, and Nod

Classic Cat Names

Sometimes it's hard to improve on tradition. While the new-fangled, fancy, exotic names may draw you in initially, you may find yourself getting back to basics—why not the much-loved Mittens, for example? Or even the quintessential Ginger? The names on this list have stood the test of time and may serve your cat well, too.

- ❏ Alley
- ❏ Amber
- ❏ Angel
- ❏ Ash
- ❏ Ashley
- ❏ Blacky
- ❏ Blackjack
- ❏ Blinky
- ❏ Blondie
- ❏ Boots
- ❏ Buddy
- ❏ Britches
- ❏ Brushtail
- ❏ Buttercup
- ❏ Butterscotch
- ❏ Calico
- ❏ Cameo
- ❏ Checkers
- ❏ Callie

- ❏ Caramel
- ❏ Cheshire
- ❏ Chester
- ❏ Chase
- ❏ Cinnamon
- ❏ Cleo
- ❏ Cleopatra
- ❏ Copper
- ❏ Copy Cat
- ❏ Cookie
- ❏ Cricket
- ❏ Daisy
- ❏ Domino
- ❏ Dot
- ❏ Ember
- ❏ Esmerelda
- ❏ Felicia
- ❏ Feather
- ❏ Felix
- ❏ Frisky

- ❏ Fudge
- ❏ Ginger
- ❏ Gypsy
- ❏ Hobie
- ❏ Jade
- ❏ Jasmine
- ❏ Kitty
- ❏ Licky
- ❏ Lucy
- ❏ Magic
- ❏ Marmalade
- ❏ Meow Meow
- ❏ Merlin
- ❏ Mew Mew
- ❏ Mewy
- ❏ Midnight
- ❏ Milky
- ❏ Miss Kitty

- ❏ Miss Priss
- ❏ Missy
- ❏ Misty
- ❏ Mittens
- ❏ Mitzy
- ❏ Molly
- ❏ Morris
- ❏ Mother Tabbyskins
- ❏ Muffin
- ❏ Muffy
- ❏ Norton
- ❏ Oscar
- ❏ Pandora
- ❏ Patches
- ❏ Pepper
- ❏ Pitch
- ❏ Precious
- ❏ Princess
- ❏ Prissy
- ❏ Purdy
- ❏ Purry
- ❏ Puss
- ❏ Puss Puss
- ❏ Ruby
- ❏ Scat
- ❏ Scotchy
- ❏ Shadow
- ❏ Slippers
- ❏ Sooty
- ❏ Snowball
- ❏ Spicy
- ❏ Spook
- ❏ Spooky
- ❏ Swat
- ❏ Tabby
- ❏ Tabitha
- ❏ Taffy
- ❏ Tailchaser
- ❏ Teddy
- ❏ Tibbs
- ❏ Tibby
- ❏ Tiger
- ❏ Tiger Lily
- ❏ Tigger
- ❏ Toby
- ❏ Toffee
- ❏ Tom
- ❏ Topaz
- ❏ Whiskers
- ❏ Whiskey

The Cat's Meow

S till having trouble deciding on a name? Check out the Feline Fabulous 40, the top cat names these days, as chosen by fellow cat lovers in the U.S., Canada, the U.K., Australia, and New Zealand. Perhaps not surprisingly, traditional names and names from movie or TV cats continue to be popular, as does the eponymous "Kitty." You can't argue with success—these are names any cat would be proud to answer to (if she answers at all).

She Cats

1. ❑ Sassy
2. ❑ Misty
3. ❑ Missy
4. ❑ Princess
5. ❑ Samantha
6. ❑ Kitty
7. ❑ Puss
8. ❑ Fluffy
9. ❑ Molly
10. ❑ Daisy
11. ❑ Ginger
12. ❑ Midnight
13. ❑ Precious
14. ❑ Maggie
15. ❑ Lucy

16. ❑ Cleo
17. ❑ Whiskers
18. ❑ Chloe
19. ❑ Sophie
20. ❑ Lily
21. ❑ Coco
22. ❑ Boo
23. ❑ Callie
24. ❑ Sadie
25. ❑ Jessie
26. ❑ Jasmine
27. ❑ Nala
28. ❑ Snowball
29. ❑ Angel
30. ❑ Muffin

31. ❑ Pumpkin
32. ❑ Pepper
33. ❑ Baby
34. ❑ Zoe
35. ❑ Peaches
36. ❑ Holly
37. ❑ Dusty
38. ❑ Katie
39. ❑ Sasha
40. ❑ Scooter

He Cats

1. ☐ Max
2. ☐ Sam
3. ☐ Tigger
4. ☐ Tiger
5. ☐ Sooty
6. ☐ Smokey
7. ☐ Lucky
8. ☐ Patch
9. ☐ Simba
10. ☐ Smudge
11. ☐ Oreo
12. ☐ Milo
13. ☐ Oscar
14. ☐ Oliver
15. ☐ Buddy
16. ☐ Boots
17. ☐ Harley
18. ☐ Gizmo
19. ☐ Charlie
20. ☐ Toby
21. ☐ Jake
22. ☐ Sebastian
23. ☐ Puffy
24. ☐ Bailey
25. ☐ Buster
26. ☐ Tom
27. ☐ Rocky
28. ☐ Jack
29. ☐ Felix
30. ☐ Spike
31. ☐ Simon
32. ☐ Taz
33. ☐ Rusty
34. ☐ Merlin
35. ☐ Monty
36. ☐ Dusty
37. ☐ Casper
38. ☐ Mittens
39. ☐ Pepper
40. ☐ Blackie

Index